Nihilism, Art, Technology

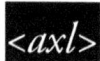

© Copyright 2011 Sven-Olov Wallenstein and Axl Books.

All rights reserved. No part of this publication may be reproduced or transmitted in any form or by any means, electronic or mechanical, including photocopy, recording, or any information storage and retrieval system, without permission in writing from the publisher.

Axl Books
Box 19009
104 32 Stockholm
Sweden
www.axlbooks.com
info@axlbooks.com

ISBN 978-91-86883-01-0

Nihilism, Art, Technology
SVEN-OLOV WALLENSTEIN

AXL BOOKS

Note to the Second Edition
For the second edition a few minor changes have been made. Apart from correcting printing errors, I have occasionally added a few words or phrases, and clarified some obscure sentences. The substance, however, remains the same.

Contents

Nihilism, Art, Technology	ix
Introduction	ix
1. Art and Technology	1
1.1. Photography and Painting	4
1.2. From Futurism to Constructivism	11
1.3. Space, Time, and Interpenetration	18
2. The Destruction of Aesthetics	25
2.1. Benjamin and the Technology of Reproduction	30
2.2. Jünger and the Metaphysics of the Worker	37
2.3. Heidegger and the Origin of the Work of Art	42
2.4. Destruction and Beyond	54
3. The Essence of Technology	63
3.1. The Essence of Technology	63
3.2. Building Thinking	73
3.3. Conflict of Interpretations: Three Ways of Reading	78
4. Reading Silence: The Case of Mies	85
4.1. Mies as Paradigm Case	85
4.2. A Brief Digression on Words	90
4.3. Negative Thought and Negative Dialectics	92
4.4. A Multiplicity of Silences	101
4.5. Crossing the Line	107

Nihilism, Art, Technology

Introduction

The following pages are intended as an introduction to selections assembled from two previously published books, which together were presented as a compilation thesis in theoretical philosophy at Stockholm University. Three of the four texts chosen were chapters from the volume *Essays, Lectures* (2007)—"Modernism and Technology," "The Destruction of Aesthetics: Benjamin, Jünger, Heidegger," and "Towards the Essence of Technology: Heidegger and the Case of Architecture"—and the fourth was the integrality of a smaller book entitled *The Silences of Mies* (2008). Although these texts dealt with the same topic, i.e. the role of technology in the formation of the artistic avant-garde, along with various forms of philosophical reflection on the development of the avant-garde, with particular emphasis on Heidegger, they were not originally written in order to provide one sustained argument, which is what the following pages shall supply. The particularities of this situation of writing might engender some of the oddities of the text at hand: it is neither simply an introductory chapter in a book, nor a work that develops an argument on its own, yet it is presented as an autonomous publication, and must somehow be able to justify its independent existence. On the one hand, it must provide a synthesis of the other texts, and present a synoptic perspective on an argument that remained implicit during the initial act of writing, and it must do so by zooming out from the small-scale texture of the previous works; on the other hand, it must at times fill in the blanks by providing scholarly references and discussions that were missing in the original publications,[1] and this it can only do by an opposite movement: zooming into the fabric, or more precisely the lacunae, of certain parts.

The overarching question is the interrelation of technology, the artistic avant-garde, and philosophical thought. From the very outset such a question blurs the line between art history, philosophy, and perhaps several other disciplines as well, and I will argue that there are good reasons for this—specifically, that the philosophical reflection on art and the arts, as it has evolved during the course of the 20th century, cannot be separated from the transformations in the arts themselves, just as these transformations within the arts cannot be properly grasped unless they are seen in relation to the vast technological transformations wrought upon our lifeworld.

Starting in the first chapter with a reading of three paradigmatic cases of the interplay between art and technology—the invention of photography and the way it caused a profound upheaval of the system of the fine arts, the historical shift from Futurism to Constructivism, and finally the interpretation of technology in debates on architectural theory in the 1920s and 1930s—the thesis proceeds to a second chapter dealing with an interpretation of three philosophical responses to this development, those found in Walter Benjamin, Martin Heidegger, and Ernst Jünger. Despite their being located all over the political spectrum, they nevertheless share a certain avant-garde sensibility.

---

1. In the following, references to and discussions of secondary literature will focus on texts that are not mentioned in the previously published works. In some cases however it has not been possible to discuss secondary literature systematically without sacrificing clarity. Unless otherwise indicated, all translations are my own.

The third chapter focuses on Heidegger in particular, and the way technology is understood in his postwar writings. Here I suggest that we can see a retreat from his positions in the mid- 1930s, which, although in many respects ambivalent and hesitant, were characterized by a certain heroic stance, with a horizon constituted by the question of whether art has the possibility of once more constituting a world in the sense of the Greek *polis*, or whether it remains under the verdict enounced by Hegel, that it is "a thing of the past." Re-reading Heidegger's reflections on technology, we can discern a different answer to the question of whether "great art" is still possible, even though it is only implicit in Heidegger's own texts: great art is an art that acknowledges the withdrawal of building, dwelling, and language.

The fourth and final chapter develops this question in relation to the work of an individual artist, the architect Mies van der Rohe. The choice of this example is by no means fortuitous. Mies's architecture has long since been the privileged object of philosophical traditions that draw on both Heidegger and Critical Theory, and has been perceived by many as an exemplary case of a work that introjects, reflects on, and thereby allows us to gain a free relation to the essence of technology. In my discussion of these interpretations, I pose the question of how the silence—the withdrawal of language, sense, aesthetic perception—that is often ascribed to them as a precondition for their critical potential should in fact be understood. This amounts to an understanding of the interrelation of nihilism, art, and technology as a field of constant modulation where none of these parameters is fixed, but each moves along with history, which also implies that the concepts that have been the foundation of critical theory, nature, subjectivity, experience, even being in Heidegger's sense, must in turn be subject to a historical analysis that acknowledges them as ongoing processes of construction, and that also accounts for the capacity of technologies and artistic practices to intervene in the formation of philosophical concepts.

•

This thesis is a compilation in many senses of the term. The first drafts were written in the early 1990s, in the framework of the research project Phenomenology and Critique of Modernity, where I had the good fortune to work with Hans Ruin, Daniel Birnbaum, Dagfinn Føllesdal, Dick Haglund, Staffan Carlshamre, and the late Alexander Orlowski, who became my supervisor during the course of our research. Originally the work was intended to deal with Heidegger, Nietzsche, and the question of *nihilism*, i.e., the downfall of classical metaphysics and the way in which Nietzsche and Heidegger attempted to diagnose the prospects of a future philosophy. Soon, however, it appeared to me that the analysis of nihilism in both of these thinkers was inextricably bound up with what they perceived as a possible antidote: *art*, either as a form of will to power in Nietzsche, or as a means of access to a certain "truth of being," as in Heidegger, which is developed partly by way of a critical confrontation with Nietzsche. Thus, in a second version of the project, my perspective shifted to Heidegger's philosophy of art, and the plan was to follow its ramifications from the work in the mid-1930s on the origin of the work of art, through the various lecture courses on Nietzsche and Hölderlin, and up to the later works and their meditations on poetry, thought, and the essence of technology. Parts of this more ambitious work have been inserted here and there in summary form, in order to clarify the historical background of the project. The third stage of the project is much closer in time, and stems from my participation in the research project Technology, Nihilism, Lifeworld at the Department of

Culture and Communication, Södertörn University, where the earlier questions were once more reframed, this time by the question of *technology*. Important in this context were also the discussions in the Academy for Practice-Based Research in Architecture and Design. Together they were the source for the small book on Mies, which corresponds to this third step. In this sense, the title of this introductory text, *Nihilism, Art, Technology*, not only points to a retroactive thematic coherence, but also reflects, from a chronological point of view, the different layers of research that have gone into it.

There are no doubt several reasons why the work as it was first intended was not completed. Some of them are trivial and biographical, others remain closer to the substance of the matter. The less superficial reasons derived from a growing need to break away from a certain type of reading of Heidegger (and other philosophers), and to confront his work not only with other philosophical traditions, but also with the kind of thinking and reflection that emerges from the practices of the arts themselves. It is my deep conviction that philosophical work on art, or aesthetics (to use a term that many of the thinkers and artists dealt with here treated with deep suspicion), must proceed in close contact with works, otherwise it is doomed to remain at the level of empty formality and generality, and the *Zwiegespräch* between *Dichten* and *Denken* that Heidegger attempted becomes simply a monologue by the philosopher himself.

This need to confront philosophy with the actual practice of the arts was further highlighted by my experience of teaching in schools of art and architecture, where I learned the extent to which philosophical thinking can be enhanced by, even requires, a milieu where concepts are put to use, and that translating philosophical concepts into other spheres is not something that deprives them of their value, but is in fact what gives them value. The many colleagues and students I have encountered through the years at the School of Film and Photography and Valand School of Fine Arts, in Gothenburg, and the University College of Arts and Crafts and the Royal Institute of Technology, in Stockholm, have contributed to this insight. The same thing must be said of the editors and colleagues at the various journals with which I have been involved since the late 1980s – *Kris*, *Material*, and most recently *Site*. Writing, editing, and engaging with contributors of all kinds is a kind of thinking in action, which proved essential to the development of my thought.

For a decade, my academic life has been spent at the department of Culture and Communication at Södertörn University, where I have been lucky enough to have been able to teach philosophy and aesthetics with great colleagues and friends, with whom I have been engaged in several research projects that formed the matrix for several of the writings presented here: I would like to thank Hans Ruin, Fredrika Spindler, Marcia Sá Cavalcante-Schuback, Cecilia Sjöholm, and Sara Danius. I must also thank Helena Mattsson, with whom I once began and still continue to discuss architecture, and Brian Manning Delaney, with whom I have shared the joys of transforming German philosophical vocabularies into both Swedish and English.

A particular thanks should go to Staffan Lundgren, the editor of Axl Books, who first suggested that I put together the collection of texts that became *Essays, Lectures*, and eventually also published *The Silences of Mies*, and to Hans Ruin, Staffan Carlshamre, and Gunnar Svensson, who finally persuaded me to present some of these writings in the form of a compilation thesis. And last but not least: Jonna Bornemark, whose love and (im)patience with the pace at which my work on the thesis proceeded, evolving from a work in progress to something perhaps on the order of what Duchamp once called the "definitively unfinished," no doubt was a fundamental reason why I finally decided to present this material in its present state.

The book is dedicated to the memory of my supervisor Alexander Orlowski.

1. Art and Technology

The first text contains a general discussion of the relation between art and technology as one of the foundational structures of modernism, as it evolved from the mid-nineteenth century onwards. The discussion traverses three distinct moments: the invention of photography as a challenge to the system of the fine arts, and as something that eventually came to call into question the very idea of a work; the technological visions of futurism, and particularly constructivism, where industrial technology was incorporated into the very substance of art; and finally, the theories of space-time and interpenetration in the architectural theory of the 1920s, where the project of a possible reshaping of the basis of subjectivity and experience reached a high point.

The overarching thesis is that there is an essential and productive relation between certain parts of the avant-garde and technological development, not in the sense of a causal connection (art as the effect of some external cause, for instance technological inventions), but in the sense of a relation of *interpretation* carried out within the theoretical and practical works of artists. Given a certain level of technological development, new productive forces, inventions, and so on, the idea of a transformative artistic practice that draws on these technologies as a means to achieve a new art becomes possible. The link between art and technology can thus just as much be reversed; rather than mere effects, artistic practices often leap ahead into the future in order to imagine and even attempt to install new social relations, as in the case of Russian Constructivism, or in the interpenetration of subject and object in architectural theory.

To some extent the picture drawn here results from the selection of sources. If literary modernism had been the guiding thread, the results would no doubt have been more confusing, and the presence of a marked technophobia would have imposed itself, though literary modernism too is impregnated with modern technology, at least when read with a keen eye towards particular details and metaphors.[1] Emphasizing the visual arts and architecture however brings out more clearly what I perceive to be most philosophically productive: the idea that the impact of technology also implies a possible transformation both of the forms of art and of subjectivity itself, that it impacts those fundamental coordinates within which subjects and objects are located, and that this transformation entails not only a loss of some previous unity or coherence, but the discovery of a new space-time that in the end might unsettle both the structure of consciousness and the status of the world that it inhabits.

In the first phase, these transformations of the inherited system of the arts were perceived as a loss, and were theorized in the form of nihilism and a devaluation of values, from Turgenev to Nietzsche, although the account of the underlying reasons for this transformation varied.[2] It could also be seen as the onset of a

1. See for instance Sara Danius, *The Senses of Modernism: Technology, Perception, and Aesthetics* (Ithaca: Cornell University Press, 2002), which discusses the presence of inventions like the x-ray machine, the movie camera, the telephone, etc., in the novels of Thomas Mann, James Joyce, and Marcel Proust.
2. The first use of the term *nihilism* can be found in Jacobi, who criticizes Kant's critical philosophy, and then Fichte's absolute I, for denying the transcendence of God. For a discussion of Jacobi and early uses of the term, see Michael Allen Gillespie, *Nihilism Before Nietzsche* (Chicago: University of Chicago Press, 1995), and Paul Franks, "All or Nothing: Systematicity and Nihilism in Jacobi, Reinhold, and Maimon," in Karl Ameriks (ed.): *The Cambridge Companion to German Idealism* (Cambridge: Cambridge: University Press, 2000). Turgenev famously introduces the concept in his 1862 novel *Fathers and Sons*, through the character Bazarov, who first rejects traditional religious, humanist, and aesthetic values in the name of science, but then displays an equal dis-

logic of *fashion*,[3] within which all things substantial evaporate, as was suggested by Baudelaire, Marx, Simmel, and many others.[4] In these figures of thought, as they evolved from the middle of the 18th century onwards, nihilism and fashion posed a fundamental question: can we continue to move ahead without being guided by transcendent values, and might we in fact, precisely by virtue of this absence of foundation, be able to create a new beauty and a new art? For a long time this new beauty tended

trust of the truth claims of science. The conflict between generations—on one side the romanticism, liberalism, and European orientation of the fathers and the liberals, on the other side the young nihilists who opt for positivism and Russian nationalism—is settled through the experience of (unrequited) love, and when Bazarov finally succumbs to typhoid, a reconciliation within Christianity seems possible. The theme was picked up in Chernyshevski's *What is to Be Done?* (1862), where the eternal values of art are negated in favor of its social utility, and from there on it was transmitted to generations of writers and political activists. For a recent overview of the development of the concept of nihilism, see Bülent Diken, *Nihilism* (London: Routledge, 2009).

3. An interesting connection between technology and fashion is established by the architect Schinkel, who sees both of them as resulting in a *loss of place*. In 1826, upon returning to Berlin from his journey to England, where he had encountered the technological marvels of industrialism, he notes, "the modern age makes everything easy, it no longer believes in permanence, and has lost all sense of monumentality." This is an epoch, he continues, "where everything becomes mobile, even that which was supposed to be most durable, namely the art of building, where the word *fashion* becomes widespread in architecture, where forms, materials, and every tool can be understood as a plaything to be treated as one wants, where one is prone to try everything since nothing is in its place (*weil nichts an seinem Orte steht*), and nothing seems mandatory." Cited in Fritz Neumeyer, "Tektonik: Das Schauspiel der Objektivität und die Wahrheit des Architekturschauspiels," in Hans Kollhoff (ed.): *Über Tektonik in der Baukunst* (Braunschweig: Vieweg & Sohn, 1993), 59. This *threatening* idea of fashion would, just like the idea of technology, become transformed into an instrumental one in the beginning of the 20th century, where the question is no longer *whether* architecture resembles fashion, but *what type* of fashion it should choose as its model, as can be seen in the writings of Adolf Loos and Le Corbusier. For further discussion, see Mark Wigley, *White Walls, Designer Dresses* (Cambridge, Mass.: MIT, 1995).

4. The classic discussion of this trope is Marshall Berman, *All That Is Solid Melts Into Air: The Experience of Modernity* (New York: Simon and Schuster, 1982).

to display a backward-looking quality, since it was often based on a possible rebirth of antiquity, as we can see in Baudelaire and Nietzsche, who both rejected, each in different ways, those aspects of modernity that were determined by technology, even though they were fundamentally conditioned by it.

The advent of the historical avant-garde brings about a shift in this constellation, in the sense that the new world that it hopes shall emerge out of the downfall of the idols must not only incorporate technology, but even merge with it, which implies that the inherited fine arts as well as our aesthetic relation to them must be transformed. The question of how this relates to the previous diagnoses of nihilism is however not simple, as we will see. For Nietzsche, nihilism spans the whole of the Western tradition, although his preferred source is Christianity; in Heidegger this genealogy becomes even more far-reaching, and nihilism is reinterpreted as the basic structure of the whole of Western metaphysics, so that Nietzsche's diagnosis and its various modernist sequels will appear as its last and consummate form, and later as the next-to-last step, to be succeeded by the advent of modern technology where the nothingness of being is finally realized. For Heidegger, nihilism cannot be countered in the Nietzschean way, by the creation of new values that seems to borrow its model from artistic production. It can only be overcome by being traversed and assumed in its most radical figure, although art in Heidegger, too, holds a crucial and strategic position.

1.1. Photography and Painting

The first step is the crisis of painting in the face of the invention of photography, in which the idea of the subjective and expressive quality of image making, and, implicitly, the hierarchy between the *artes liberales* and *artes mechanicae* that still informs the concept of fine art, underwent a profound upheaval. What started out as a shift in the understanding of the ontology of the image—or more precisely, the emerging possibility of stating the question of the image in ontological terms, so that the "*what* is..." gradually superseded, or was seen as preceding, the questions of beauty, composition, etc.—was eventually generalized so as to encompass not only painting, but also sculpture, literature, music and finally art *in general*, and it would become an essential feature of modern art as an aesthetic as well as ontological unrest.[5]

In the initial debates, which primarily took place with reference to painting, two lines of argumentation can be discerned. In the first, the discovery of the tactile, manual, and physical properties of the surface could be taken as a *resistance* to the advent of technology, and the modernist quest for the self-definition of art would in this case amount to a reaction against the technological determination of experience. The encounter with photography as a medium that mechanized image production was perceived as a dismantling of subjectivity and imagination, even as the end of painting as such, as epitomized in Paul Delaroche's hyperbolic outcry in 1839: "From today, painting is dead,"[6] a statement which recurs throughout the literature, even though it appears to be the result of a retroactive fantasy.

5. This is how we can read Mallarmé's defense of Manet, when the latter was refused by the Salon jury in 1874: the task of the jury, Mallarmé says, is not to judge whether a painting is good or not, but simply whether it is a painting at all. See Mallarmé, "Le jury de peinture pour 1874 et M. Manet," *Écrits sur l'art*, ed. Michel Draguet (Paris: Flammarion, 1998), 297ff.
6. Delaroche was in fact one of those to whom Arago turned for an official report on the new invention, and he seemed to have belonged to those who saw photography as a highly useful tool; see Stephen Bann, *Paul Delaroche: History Painted* (London: Reaktion, 1997), 226f, 264. Delaroche's report in fact claims that "Daguerre's process [...] completely satisfies all the requirement of Art, and carries so far the perfection of certain of its conditions that it will become even for the most skilful painters a subject of observation and study" (cited in Bann, 264).

In the second line of argument, the emergence of mechanized images was understood in the opposite way, and photography now in fact *liberates* the imagination by redirecting it toward the essentials of art. In the words of the contemporary critic Francis Wey: "By reducing that which is inferior to art to nothing, the heliograph sets art on a course towards new achievements, and by summoning the artist back to nature it draws him closer to an infinitely rich source of inspiration."[7]

These two claims were in fact not seen as entirely opposed, and we should rather speak of a dialectic within which the very terrain of the debate was gradually shifted. Realist artists like Courbet could sometimes excel in almost mechanical visions where photography merged with a positivist idea of sheer facts, while the early photographers in many cases revisited an academic pictorial tradition in order to attain that very status of fine art, which painters were increasingly questioning. Here we find something like a mimetic rivalry, played out within a discourse of a transformed notion of *mimesis*: if the quest for painterly autonomy could be based on the intuition that the essence of painting is entirely foreign to the photographic, then it is just as true that the historical emergence of photography was *required* for this essence to appear; the domain of the visible that painting claimed had to emancipate itself from the seductive lure of technology, could not do without it as its negative other. In this sense, the modernity of painting was both made possibly by the new image technology and haunted by a suspicion that

---

7. Francis Wey, "Du naturalisme dans l'art," published in *La lumière*, April 6, 1851, rpr. in André Rouillé, *La photographie en France: textes & controverses; une anthologie, 1816–1871* (Paris: Macula, 1989), 116. Wey was one of the first who took photography seriously as a critic, and his writings in *La lumière* were instrumental in providing the new art with institutional authority; see Emmanuel Hermange, "Aspects and Uses of Ekphrasis in Relation to Photography, 1816–1860," *Journal of European Studies* 30 (2000).

the new terrain it was conquering was in fact only negatively determined. The arrival of abstraction at the outset of the 20th century could in this sense be understood both as the final discovery of what painting had been since the beginning, and as a last stance, beyond which painting had to be abandoned in favor of other forms of practice that would be able to interiorize mechanical and serial (re)production into their very substance.

The first stance, which claims to uncover a primordial perceptual dimension in and through painting, can be taken to underlie Cézanne's famous claim to show us "the truth in painting,"[8] through a descent into the genesis of the visible that takes its cues from the pure *sensations colorantes*, just as it informs Paul

---

8. Paul Cézanne, letter to Émile Bernard, October 25, 1905, in *Correspondence*, ed. John Rewald (Paris: Grasset, 1937), 315. This reading of Cézanne is of course by no means undisputed from an art-historical point of view. I refer here primarily to Merleau-Ponty's interpretation, above all in "Le doute de Cézanne" (1945) in *Sens et non-sens* (Paris: Nagel, 1948), which I take to be a model for a certain phenomenological account of art as a way to resist technology and retrieve a more originary connection to the world of the senses. Other philosophically oriented interpretations of early abstraction are surely just as possible, as for instance that found in Jean-François Lyotard, "Freud selon Cézanne," in *Les dispositifs pulsionnels* (Paris: Bourgeois, 1980). Lyotard opposes the moment of *destruction* of sense and the *muteness* and *opacity* in Cézanne's last paintings, read in terms of the disruptive "figurality" of libidinal economy to what he sees as the "gullibility of the phenomenologist" with respect to the idea that painting would give us the truth of some primordial foundation of meaning. For a comprehensive interpretations of Cézanne's claim, which locates it in the context of the discourse on nature in the latter half of the 19th century (for, regardless of the above-mentioned, presumably interminable conflicts of interpretation, one must bear in mind that Cézanne's letter to Bernard in fact continues: "Tout est, en art surtout, théorie développée et appliquée au contact de la nature"), see Denis Coutagne, *Cézanne en vérité(s): "Je vous dois la vérité en peinture et je vous la dirai"* (Arles: Actes Sud, 2006). See also the contributions in Denis Coutagne et al. (eds.): *Ce que Cézanne donne à penser: Actes du colloque d'Aix-en-Provence juillet 2006* (Paris: Gallimard, 2008). For a collection of assessments of Merleau-Ponty's writings on painting, see *The Merleau-Ponty Aesthetics Reader: Philosophy and Painting*, ed. Galen A. Johnson (Evanston, Ill.: Northwestern University Press, 1993).

Klee's later suggestion that the task of the modern artist is not to "render the visible," but to "render visible" ("Kunst gibt nicht das Sichtbare wieder, sondern macht sichtbar"),[9] i.e., to access a dimension of things that precedes our common perception. The task of painting in this version is to save us from the supremacy of subject and object by opening a domain prior to both of them, a new Visibility from out of which everyday entities emerge.

The second stance, which emerges in the period around the First World War, instead assumes that painting must accept that technology has deprived it not only of its old mimetic function, but also dispelled the idea that it could reach a more true, profound, or elevated reality. Painting must become a material entity, and it must assert its presence in the world as a thing—which in some cases, although not in all, was the last necessary step to be taken before abandoning it, as in Russian Constructivism.

Just as little as in the first clash between academic painting and photography did this conflict of interpretations entail any clear-cut division. To a large extent the dialectic of modernist painting evinces the mutual implication and even inextricable entanglement of these two positions, where the emphasis on manual dexterity, brushwork, gesture, etc., quickly passes over into experiments with tools and techniques that question the

9. Paul Klee, "Schöpferische Konfession," drafted in 1918 under the title "Über Grafik," first published 1920 in Kasimir Edschmid's *Tribüne der Kunst und Zeit*, rpr. in Klee, *Das bildnerische Denken: Form- und Gestaltungslehre*, ed. Jürg Spiller (Basel: Schwabe, 1981), 76. Klee's statement has been just as abundantly commented on from a philosophical point of view as Cézanne's. For a discussion of the historical context of Klee's claim, see Mark Roskill, *Klee, Kandinsky, and the Thought of Their Time: A Critical Perspective* (Urbana and Chicago: University of Illinois Press, 1992). Similarly to Cézanne, Klee's statement is ultimately rooted in a perception of nature, which in Klee's case involves a cosmological vision; see Reiner Wiehl, "Philosophie der Kunst und Philosophie der Natur im Bildwerk Paul Klees," in Guttorm Fløistad (ed.): *Aesthetics and Philosophy of Art* (Dordrecht: Springer, 2007), which draws Klee close to the philosophy of nature of Whitehead.

expressivity of the former techniques, often in one and the same artist's work. This shifting and multi-faceted engagement with objecthood indicates the inaptitude of a casual explanation: there is no single technological change of which modernist painting would be the result; rather, we should attempt to grasp a whole technological milieu in which certain components could be interpreted as incitements for a rethinking of art.

It is precisely this entanglement that we can locate in Baudelaire's famous Salon essay from 1859, "Le public moderne et la photographie." The poet here attacks photography for introducing a foreign technological element into art, which impinges on the "sphere of the intangible and imaginary," replacing it with a cult of an "industrial process," a "purely material process" that appeals to "the stupidity of the masses."[10] On the other hand, as many scholars have shown, Baudelaire's aesthetic sensibility is shaped by the experience of the crowd, and when he the same year describes the activity of the "the painter of modern life" in the guise of the illustrator Constantin Guys, his writing is shot through with photographic imagery. Immersing himself in the spectacle of the crowd as if it were "an immense reservoir of electrical energy," Guys becomes a "mirror as vast as the crowd itself,"[11] and then he withdraws into a nocturnal solitude, as if developing in a photographic fashion the images he has received and imbuing them with his imagination. Only in conjunction can these two movements, immersion and withdrawal, connected in the same way as the "fugitive" and the "eternal" element in mo-

10. "Salon de 1859, II: Le public moderne et la photographie," in *Curiosités esthétiques* (Lausanne: La Guilde du Livre, 1949), 267–69; English translation in Alan Trachtenberg (ed.): *Classic Essays on Photography* (New Haven: Leete's Island Books, 1980), 86–88.
11. *Le peintre de la vie moderne* III ("Homme du monde, homme des foules et enfant"), in *L'art romantique*, 86f; English translation by Jonathan Mayne in *The Painter of Modern Life and Other Essays* (London: Phaidon Press,1995), 9f.

dernity, constitute the new beauty in its twofold structure, both ephemeral fashion and immutable Idea. In this sense, Baudelaire's emphatic rejection of photography is already made possible by a photographical experience. Similarly, his deeply ambivalent letter to Manet six years later is already impregnated by the logic of fashion that condemns each expression to be displaced by the next one in line, when he first advises the painter to disregard the public scorn heaped upon him, since others of equal and even greater stature have met with the same reactions ("Croyez-vous que vous soyez le premier homme dans ce cas? Avez-vous plus de génie que Chateaubriand et que Wagner?), but then, in a curious twist, proposes that things will *just get worse*: "you are only the first in the degeneration of your art" ("Vous n'êtes que le premier dans la décrépitude de votre art").[12]

Baudelaire's painter of modern life, who is no doubt more a projection of the poet-author himself as a visionary seer of modernity than a portrait of a semi-famous illustrator of the period, attempts to retain a traditional image of the artist as endowed with a higher faculty of imagination that transfigures the images of quotidian reality into Art, but the new experience yielded by urban space, crowds, and technological media, will soon make the tools proposed for this task obsolete. It is this conclusion

12. Letter to Manet, May 11, 1865, *Correspondance*, eds. Claude Pichois and Jean Ziegler (Paris: Gallimard/Pléiade, 1973), vol. II, 496f. The exact significance of this phrase is debated, as is the extent to which Baudelaire sides with Manet. Here it may suffice to note that Baudelaire's phrase, as Daniel Payot suggests, points to an experience of corruption, where works become incapable of idealizing and instead descend into the chaotic and non-bounded texture of matter. See Payot, *L'objet-fibule: Les petites attaches de l'art contemporain* (Paris: L'Harmattan, 1997), 53. A similar idea underlies the re-reading of modern art in terms of the "formless," proposed by Yve-Alain Bois and Rosalind Krauss, in *Formless: A User's Guide* (New York: Zone Books, 1997), which too begins from Manet, although read in terms of the operation of "slippage" suggested by Bataille in *Manet, Œuvres complètes*, vol. 9 (Paris: Gallimard, 1979).

that will be drawn in the next moment that will be highlighted, the transformation from Futurism to Constructivism in the 1910s and 1920s, where the incorporation of technology into art occurs at a more profound level than that of the image as a mode of representation.

1.2. From Futurism to Constructivism

This second step is the discussion of the analytic and rational character of art that unfolded from Futurism through Constructivism to Productionism. Futurism, in all of its ecstatic and flamboyant praise of technology, remained largely within a mimetic and representational paradigm of production, which is indicated by its rapid return to traditional artistic forms and cultural policies, most evident in Marinetti's own attempts to enroll Futurism in the creation of a new "sacred art."[13] The Futurist artist was still modeled on the singular *genius*, caught up in a double-bind in relation to a culture and an audience that he could only set out to shock, or even destroy (as in Marinetti's prospect for aerial bombing, in "Contro Venezia passatista"),[14] and not yet the *worker*, in tune with the demands of the new masses and their collective material culture.

This decisive incorporation of technology was first enacted

13. For a discussion of the political context of this series of retractions, which were initiated at the Futurist congress in 1924 when Marinetti decides to accept the monarchy as sign of political unity, then decides that a historical compromise with the Vatican is necessary and publicly declares his Catholic faith, and finally curates a Futurist section at the 1931 Mostra Internazionale di Arte Sacra, see Günther Berghaus, *Futurism and Politics: Between Anarchist Rebellion and Fascist Reaction, 1909–1944* (Providence: Berghahn Books, 1996), 245ff.
14. The manifesto, which opposes the putrefying past of Venice to Milan as the city of the future, is dated April 27, 1910, and was also signed by Boccioni, Carrà, and Russolo. For the context, and for the Futurist image of the city in general, see Christine Poggi, *Inventing Futurism: The Art and Politics of Artificial Optimism* (Princeton, NJ.: Princeton University Press, 2009), chap. 3 (on Venice, 67f).

in Russian Constructivism. This was a radicalization and generalization of the earlier debates on painting, and led to an attempt to rethink the whole concept of art on the basis of industrial production, but also to the idea that the very structure of subjectivity could be transformed. In this phase, abstraction was understood neither as an exploration of sensible qualities, nor as the ascent into a realm of essences, but as a way to gain mastery over the technical production process. Beginning as a quest for the purity of art forms (which later, in postwar formalist criticism, in a rather anachronistic fashion was taken as the key to these earlier movements), this development soon led beyond the inherited artistic means of production—the canvas, the stretcher, tools for drawing, color and pigment, etc.—which were now understood as historically produced and thus contingent limitations that could and ought to be discarded.

The continued relevance and even superiority of painting claimed by, for instance, Malevich and Kandinsky, can be taken as an intermediary position, as is seen by the role played by Kandinsky in the Bauhaus, and by Malevich in the debates around Constructivism. As a path towards a universal theory of form, painting could fulfill a preparatory function, but in the end its ties to nineteenth-century culture and aesthetics forced it into obsolescence. In the passage from a "laboratory" phase into the full-blown program of Productionism, Malevich's "objectless world" and his quest for "pure beauty" came to appear as idealist and retrograde in comparison to the more radical materialist and utilitarian stance of an artist like Tatlin. While the primordial void of Suprematism, out of which new forms were supposed to be generated, rejected mimesis and emphasized a radical and as yet undetermined future of art,[15] it remained a

15. For a discussion of the rejection of *mimesis* and the idea of a radical future, see Andrew Benjamin, "Malevich and the Avant-Garde," in Benjamin, *Art, Mimesis and the Avant-Garde* (London: Routledge, 1991).

spiritual interpretation that gave a priority to painting as a traditional medium, whereas Tatlin's colors and shapes were nothing but physical facts, part of a "culture of materials" supposed to act directly in real space. Decisive in this context are the debates on the concept of "facture" (*faktura*): gradually shifting from a quality that pertains to the hand, to "touch," and its capacity to infuse matter with a spiritual significance, to a sense of objective structural and tectonic order, we can see how this concept transforms the nineteenth-century question whether *representation* could be mechanized into a more profound reorganization of the very fabric of the picture as a pure material object, beyond the problem of mimesis.

The trajectory of Rodchenko can be taken as paradigmatic for this development. From his earlier attempts to develop a grammar of painting on the basis of an isolation of elements like color and drawing, through the presentation of monochrome surfaces proclaiming the farewell to painting, to his collaborative efforts with Mayakovsky in the hope of creating not only a new type of advertising, but a whole new visual culture, he was ceaselessly engaged in an attempt to rethink art on the basis of new production technologies. His famous three monochrome canvases, shown for the first time in the fall of 1921, had already prompted the critic Nikolai Tarabukin to claim, a few months before, that "the last painting has been painted,"[16] but they

16. This was the title of a lecture given in the fall of 1921, later included in Tarabukin's 1923 book *From the Easel to the Machine*, where he develops a systematic theory of the evolutionary path of modernist painting, which on the one hand leads towards an "irreversible dissolution of painting into its constitutive moments," and on the other hand towards a "demise of painting as a typical art form" (cited from the French translation, *Le dernier tableau* [Paris: Champ Libre, 1972], 33). On Tarabukin's theory of art, see Maria Gough, *The Artist as Producer: Russian Constructivism in Revolution* (Berkeley: University of California Press, 2005), and idem, "Tarabukin, Spengler, and the Art of Production," *October*, vol. 93 (Summer, 2000). Gough connects Tarabukin's understanding of technology to Spengler, and argues that this made it possible for him

also gestured toward the emergence of an "artist-constructor" who takes the decisive step into "production," and for whom the industrial logic displaces the priority of the individual artifact, as is evidenced by the manifesto of the First Constructivist Working Group, signed by Rodchenko, Varvara Stepanova, and Alexei Gan the following fall in 1922.[17] The step "into production" could on one level preserve all the lessons learned from the analytical de-composition of painting (line, *faktura*, construction, tectonics, etc.), concepts that had also been developed with great analytical rigor in various formalist art theories. But even though the formalists carried out a similar analysis of the limits of traditional aesthetic appreciation, and favored a technical understanding of the work as produced through transparent and technical means applied to a historically changing raw material (words, images, and their inherited grammar), as in Shklovsky's conception of "Art as Device," not all of them embraced a wholesale rejection of the fine arts as such—in fact, Shklovsky's demand that the artist must "make the stone stony" by removing the "algebraization" of knowledge has a strong resemblance to the phenomenological quest for originary intuitions and the "things themselves," and it draws on a long series of influences leading back through Bergson to Novalis and German Romanticism[18]—whereas the technicist and utilitarian

> to theorize Constructivism as an art able to face the central paradox of industrial modernity, "the loss of the discrete object," and instead opt for the "'laying bare' of the process of production itself as the essence of the Constructivists' future endeavor" ("Tarabukin, Spengler, and the Art of Production," 108).

17. Translated in Charles Harrison and Paul Wood (eds.): *Art in Theory 1900–1990* (Oxford: Blackwell, 1992), 317f.
18. On Husserl and Russian formalism, see Victor Ehrlich, *Russian Formalism* (The Hague: Mouton, 1980). For the connection to Bergson, see James M. Curtis, "Bergson and Russian Formalism," *Comparative Literature*, vol. 28, No. 2 (Spring, 1976): 109–121. Tzvetan Todorov points to the connection to Novalis and Romanticism in *Critique de la critique: Un roman d'apprentissage* (Paris: Seuil, 1984).

imperative of productionism demanded that they must be applied to a much larger field that extends beyond the aesthetic and institutional frames imposed by the idea of "fine art."

This step was however taken by other formalist theorists, as for instance Osip Brik, in essays like "Into Production" (1923), and most emphatically by Boris Arvatov. In Arvatov, we can see the social and political conclusions that would seem to follow from the step beyond the formal-structural analysis of the closure of traditional art forms proposed by earlier theorists: art must leave formal experiments behind and become one with life and work, it must enter into schools and factories. Avant-garde activities, he argues, form a "historical bridge" that must indeed be traversed but then left behind if the new culture is to be born. In his 1926 collection of essays, *Art and Production*, Arvatov sketches how this step is to be taken through the transformation of artistic techniques, the emphasis on collaborative work, and the transformation of the idea of the individual artist and his spontaneity, all of which leads to a new organization of everyday life, understood as an organic and fluid entity which continually must undo and even abolish itself (so that in the end, even the very concept "everyday life," *byt*, must be abandoned, Arvatov suggests).

For this a new persona is required, an artist-engineer (*hudoznik-inzener*) who must transcend both the artist and the engineer in their traditional forms, since both of them are results of a division of labor that separates hand and intellect, art and science, subjectivity and rational planning, etc. Only then can the new culture be constructed, a culture which in the end knows no difference between the producer and the consumer, and where everything is subsumed under the category "work" or "production," which oscillates between a self-organizing organic unity ("the free conscious will of the collective," in Arvatov's words), and a more disciplinary version, as in the poet Aleksei Gastev's theory of a "scientific organization of work," which draws heavily on Taylorism.

Whether this amounts to a demiurgic vision of the artist, who after the death of God and the downfall of tradition claims to remodel all of society on the basis of his own superior will, or in fact provides space for a more complex model of individual and collective, is a question that cannot be easily settled: the artist in the individual sense was indeed supposed to be superseded, although the model of the artist (often fused with that of the technician and the engineer) was retained. As we will see, the alternative proposed by Benjamin, between an "aestheticizing of politics" and a "politicizing of art" may be insufficient to account for this transformation, since both of these positions quickly pass over into each other and often become virtually indistinguishable. The attack on the idea of aesthetic autonomy rather implies that politics becomes subsumed under an enlarged theory of *poiesis*, i.e. a "fiction of the political"[19] in the sense of a *fabrication*, which absorbs aspects of art while still claiming to supersede it.

This ambiguity is also reflected on the level of individual experiences and desires. Rather than simply a way to eradicate individuality in a straightforward process of rationalization, as it has been understood by many historians, a considerable amount of Constructivist fantasy was in fact geared toward a kind of re-

19. I borrow this understanding of fiction from Philippe Lacoue-Labarthe, *La fiction du politique: Heidegger, l'art et la politique* (Paris: Christian Bourgois, 1988). The idea of the political order as a *Gesamtkunstwerk* is part of this tradition, whose genealogy in one sense would take us all the way back to Plato (as is argued by Lacoue-Labarthe), although the decisive turn occurred in German Idealism. For a detailed account of this tradition, see Roger Fornoff, *Die Sehnsucht nach dem Gesamtkunstwerk: Studien zu einer ästhetischen Konzeption der Moderne* (Hildesheim: Olms, 2004). Odo Marquard stresses the role of Schelling in his catalog essay "Gesamtkunstwerk und Identitätssystem," in Harald Szeeman (ed.): *Der Hang zum Gesamtkunstwerk*, exh. cat. (Aarau: Sauerländer, 1983); the exhibition was shown in Kunsthaus Zürich in 1983, and prominently featured a reconstruction of Schwitter's Merzbau, as well as many other modern avatars of the "total" work of art.

structuring of subjectivity, in a way that would provide it with a certain freedom, or even *design* a space of freedom, all of which engendered a particularly complex and fantasmatic relation to technology. A paradigm case of this is the Workers Club, designed by Rodchenko for the Russian Pavilion at the Exposition Internationale des Arts Décoratifs et Industriels in Paris 1925. A first sight little more than a low-tech version of functionalist modernism, it can in fact be read as a strategy for highlighting a bodily dimension and encouraging an tactile and erotic investment in objects: rather than simply a *negation* of subjectivity, it was a strategy for *reshaping* it on the basis of a new assemblage of man and machine, perhaps as a way to introduce Nietzsche's famous (although highly ambivalent) image of man as "the animal whose nature has as not yet been fixed" (*das noch nicht festgestellte Tier*)[20] into a distinctly Communist avant-garde project, or to

20. When Nietzsche speaks of this peculiar animal, he refers to it on the one hand as something failed and lacking in strength, on the other hand as a set of possibilities: "there is a surplus of failures, of the sick, the degenerate, the fragile, of those who are bound to suffer; the successful cases are, among men too, always the exception, and, considering that man is the *animal whose nature has not yet been fixed*, the rare exception." *Beyond Good and Evil*, trans. R. J. Hollingdale (London: Penguin, 1972), no. 62, Nietzsche's italics. In one of the *Nachlass* notes, the negative tone prevails: "Grundsatz: das, was im Kampf mit den Thieren dem Menschen seinen Sieg errang, hat zugleich die schwierige und gefährliche krankhafte Entwicklung des Menschen mit sich gebracht. Er ist das *noch nicht festgestellte Thier*." *Nachgelassene Fragmente Frühjahr-Herbst 1884: Kritische Gesamtausgabe*, eds. Colli and Montinari, section 7, vol. 2 (Berlin and New York: Walter de Gruyter, 1974), 121. In other passages the enigmatic, even abyssal, character of the question appears again. Whether everything that we hitherto have understood as morality, humanity, compassion, etc., is nothing but an attenuation of more and profound powerful drives, which makes the "type" man into something smaller and breeds mediocrity, whether men, who in praising morality believed they were raising themselves to the status of Gods, in fact were sinking to the level of the herd, "und vielleicht das Thier 'Mensch' damit feststellen – denn bisher war der Mensch das 'nicht festgestellte Thier'"—this, Nietzsche writes, is a question that is "mein Sphinx, neben der nicht nur Ein Abgrund ist." *Nachgelassene Fragmente: Herbst 1884 bis Herbst 1885*, ibid. section 7, vol. 3, 69f. When Heidegger in his lectures

create what was in other contexts other referred to as the "New Man," whose glorious form could only appear from a new "point zero" of humanity and history.

The project for the creation of such a new man would however soon come to lead to a turn from disruptive techniques to more unitary and "realist" techniques, as can be seen in photography, visual arts, and literature. The destruction or dismantling of the aesthetic frame thus allowed politics to become the subject of the work, in all senses of the word, unleashing a force that the artists themselves were incapable of containing, and in this sense the demise and eventual condemnation of Constructivism as "formalism" was inherent in the movement's own logic from the beginning.

1.3. Space, Time, and Interpenetration

The third moment, which is in fact contemporaneous with the second, is the new determinations of space and time in architectural theory in the 1920s. From the emergence of the concept of space as a properly aesthetic, and particularly architectural concept in the 1880s and 1890s, a series of concepts were forged in order to point to the possibility of a new alloy of the organic and the technical, and to the possibility of *producing* the spacetime of experience in a way that detaches it from the subject as a form of interiority.

A key text in this shift is the 1928 book by the historian and critic Sigfried Giedion, *Bauen in Frankreich, Bauen in Eisen, Bauen*

> from 1938–39 comments on this concept in his interpretation of the second of the *Untimely Meditations*, he suggests that the underlying distinction between man as a bearer of reason and spirit, and the animal as body, indicates that Nietzsche still thinks within metaphysics, and here more precisely in a form that inverts Descartes, but he does connect this animality to technology. See Heidegger, *Zur Auslegung von Nietzsches II. unzeitgemässer Betrachtung "Vom Nutzen und Nachteil der Historie für das Leben"*. *Gesamtausgabe*, section 2, Vorlesungen 1919–1944, vol. 46 (Frankfurt am Main: Klostermann, 2003), 26, 256, 353.

in Eisenbeton, which articulates in a clear way the philosophical claims of the modern movement in architecture, and in doing so also had a profound influence on Walter Benjamin. The radical interpretation of space proposed by Giedion, welding together motifs from a discussion underway since the final third of the 19th century, and heralding the fusion of organic and the technological in terms of a new consciousness of "construction," may be read like a prism from which later developments will emerge as so many refractions. In fact, Giedion's own subsequent and more well-known work, *Space, Time and Architecture* (1941), in many respects constitutes a step back from the more radical proposals of the earlier work, above all concerning the very existence of "architecture" as a distinct art.

Tracing the development of glass and iron constructions through the 19th century, Giedion wants to locate a "constructive subconsciousness" that surfaces in the discussions on style and tectonics, and in the dialectic of core-form (technology) and art-form (aesthetic surface), which eventually was ushered into modern architecture in the breakthroughs of architects like Auguste Perret and Tony Garnier, and achieved a first state of perfection in Le Corbusier. This subconscious can now become rational construction, Giedion claims, and for him this also implies that the oppositions that structured nineteenth-century architecture, both in theory and in practice, now may enter into a new fusion, or a state of mutual "interpenetration" (*Durchdringung*). This interpenetration points both to an integration of architectural forms (volumes, floors, interior and exterior, etc.), and to a transformed social sensibility at large, within which a "common task" that unites previously separated professions and social classes begins to emerge. Eventually—and in fact, this is a shift that for Giedion in 1928 seems wholly imminent—this will render the inherited concept of architecture as a particular art obsolete, since the art of building must henceforth be understood as a way to channel and control "streams of movement," as an instrument within an overarching spatial regimentation and not as the purveyor of aesthetic forms addressed to the faculty of taste.

These ideas, both as an analysis of architectural forms and as a general vision of technology and politics, exerted a profound influence on Benjamin's reading of history as well as on his utopian visions. In the essay "Erfahrung und Armut" (1933) he suggests that modern architecture, particularly in its use of glass, presents us with a new "poverty" or even "barbarism." Benjamin associates Giedion's theories to Paul Scheerbart's 1914 manifesto *Glasarchitektur*, and develops a theory of social transparency that emphasizes the reduction of psychology and interiority in favor or spaces where we no longer "leave traces," but learn how to exist in a state of anonymity, where we exist in terms of collective "Leute" instead of individual "Menschen"—whereas Scheerbart, whose writings are imbued with an Expressionist sensibility, understands glass as a source of comfort and well-being, and rather sees the fusion of the technological and the organic as the possibility for a renewed rule of subjective pleasure and fantasy.

For Benjamin, the synthesis of the organic and the technological liberates us from a defunct and decaying culture, and it makes possible a new "Erlebnis" of poverty, which appears as a barbarism when measured by the "Erfahrung" of the past, although it in fact constitutes the condition for a positive appreciation of the emerging modes of non-auratic artistic production. In cinema, photography, and architecture, but also in modern science and engineering constructions, Benjamin sees not only the possibility for a restructuring of our perceptual and social habits, but also of a new sense of nature, as he suggest in a note in the Arcades project: "One could formulate the problem of the new art in the following way: when and how will the worlds of mechanical forms, in cinema, in the construction of machines, in the new physics, etc., appear without our help and overwhelm us, *make us conscious of what is natural in them?*"[21]

If the exchange between Giedion and Benjamin defines a crucial moment of the avant-garde between the wars, then the subsequent work of Giedion, beginning with his monumental *Space, Time and Architecture*, whose first edition appeared in 1941 and through all of its gradually expanded new editions would establish itself as the standard reference for modernist architectural theory, signifies a considerable retraction of his earlier avant-garde zeal. In this later phase Giedion's concern is to reconnect the "new tradition" to the past, bridge the gap between "rational construction" and emotional needs, and retrieve a "hidden unity" in our civilization. Once more, this unity is created by architecture, and more precisely by its treatment of space and time, although the earlier idea of interpenetration, with its radical implications for the very autonomy and existence of architecture as well as for social and political space recedes into the background. Space-time henceforth appears as a primordially *aesthetic* category, and it assumes the same organizing function as central perspective once had in the Renaissance.

The discourse on space, whose different aspects are brought together in Giedion's book, was an invention of the late 19th century, and it reached its first high point in the architectural avant-garde of the 1920s. From the first outlines of a theory of empathy in the 1870s up to August Schmarsow's groundbreaking formulas two decades later, space emerges not just as a container, but as total experience, a *Raumgefühl* that results from the interplay of the body as a zero-element and the impact of architectural form. In this sense, Schmarsow anticipates many of the themes that will

21. *Das Passagen-Werk*, *Gesammelte Schriften* (Frankfurt am Main: Suhrkamp, 1997), V, 500 (my italics).

be central in the phenomenological tradition, but he also makes possible a certain historicizing of space, so that the history of architecture, he proposes, should be written as the history of the "senses of space." If architecture is rooted in an experience of space, which in turn is founded upon the body, then this body is itself subject to change by being inscribed in those technological assemblages that induce and produce our experience of space. The project of the avant-garde as we find it in *Bauen in Frankreich*, to actively produce a new space that breaks down the barriers between subjects and objects, in order to allow for a new interpenetrating structuring of everyday life from the bottom and up, here finds one of its roots.

In *Space, Time and Architecture* this more recent historical background is however brushed aside, and Giedion instead establishes a grand historical narrative covering all of the history of culture in a vast sweeping gesture, taking us from Egypt and Greece to the present, which is now understood as a dialectical synthesis of all the moments of the past. The questioning of the very term "architecture" that resulted from the analysis in 1928 has here disappeared, and the problem now seems to be how to *consolidate* the results of a long history, and retrieve the human being of a humanism that the earlier work was calling into question. The great synthetic work of modernism that appears in *Space, Time and Architecture* is indeed beset by a doubt, and in this it opens another phase, another questioning, which attempts once more to come to terms with the *danger* of technology, to which we will return below.

2. The Destruction of Aesthetics

As we saw in the previous section, an essential task of the avant-garde consisted in fundamentally rethinking the idea of aesthetic experience. In a world permeated by technology, commodities, and violent transformations of the life-world, art, too, had to undergo a change, and the question became whether this change could amount to a return to something that had been lost, or necessarily had to embrace the new social, political, and technological forces whose consequences still hung in the balance—those "diabolical powers, whatever their message might be," that "brush up against the doors and rejoice already from the fact that they will arrive soon" as Kafka writes.[1] Is there something lodged inside the

1. Letter to Max Brod, October 25, 1923, cited in Gilles Deleuze and Félix Guattari, *Kafka: Towards a Minor Literature*, trans. Dana Polan (Minneapolis: University of Minnesota Press, 1986), 12. This citation recurs in many forms throughout Deleuze and Guattari's work, and in the case of Kafka, they suggest that we should read it as a diagnosis or a "cartography" of those lines of power and flight that would come to traverse the 20th century. This wrests the artwork free from the subjective domain and connects it to collective movements: "There isn't a subject; *there are only collective assemblages of enunciation,* and literature expresses these acts insofar as they're not imposed from without and insofar as they exist only as diabolical powers to come or revolutionary forces to be constructed" (18), "Fascism, Stalinism, Americanism, *diabolical powers that are knocking at the door* (41). Instead of creating utopian and/or dystopian vision, Kafka's method should be seen as immanent, Deleuze and Guattari propose, and it "consists in prolonging, in accelerating, a whole movement that already is traversing the social field. It operates in a virtuality that is already real without yet being actual (the diabolical powers of the future that for the moment are only brushing up against the door)" (48). My reading of the avant-garde as the possibility of transformation is indebted to these ideas, which obviously have just as much (or more) to do with Deleuze and Guattari, than with the Kafka

concept of art that would allow it to act as an antidote to nihilism, and if so, does this require that we somehow pass through the destruction of previous values as a necessary preparatory moment?

With respect to art, we can speak of a "destruction of aesthetics," in the sense that we find in Heidegger, but also in Benjamin, although with a slightly different emphasis. The destruction is not simply a negative action, but a way to liberate a possibility lying dormant in an inherited concept by dismantling—"abbauen,"[2] as Heidegger says—those sedimentations that have come to overlay it. With respect to art, this dismantling operation is carried out on the idea of aesthetic autonomy that evolved from Baumgarten to Kant, and then became one of the basic tenets of modernism, although not the only one. In opposition to this idea of autonomy, which eventually was to merge with the various doctrines of *l'art pour l'art* and symbolism at the end of the 18th century, there was always a counter-movement, beginning already in Romanticism, within which art was understood as the transformative power par excellence, capable of bringing together, in one and the same movement, the disjointed faculties of the subject as well as the fractured multiplicity of the people into a higher unity, where aesthetics and politics pass over into each other and form a highly unstable opposition.

If the avant-garde makes the claim that art should regain its power to transform the world, that it must break out of the confines of taste and aesthetic judgment, for instance by assuming

> of literary scholarship. For a discussion of Deleuze and Guattari's use of Kafka, see Ronald Bogue, *Deleuze and Guattari on Literature*, chap. 3–4.
>
> 2.   "Construction in philosophy is necessarily destruction, that is to say a de-constructing (*Abbau*) of traditional concepts carried out in a historical recursion to the tradition [...] Because destruction belongs to construction, philosophical cognition is essentially at the same time, in a certain sense, historical cognition." Heidegger, *The Basic Problems of Phenomenology*, trans. Albert Hofstadter (Bloomington: Indiana University Press, 1982), 23; *Grundprobleme der Phänomenologie, Gesamtausgabe* vol. 24 (Frankfurt am Main: Klostermann, 1975), 31.

the kind of Productionist and utilitarian attitudes that we saw in Constructivism, then this can be understood both as a rejection of autonomy, as it was worked out in the idealist tradition, and at the same time a reactivation of the Romantic promise of a supreme unity in a new context determined by industrial technology. This indicates the historical complexity of these moves, and why they cannot be explained as a linear development.

As Peter Bürger has noted, there is also an institutional setting that must be accounted for. The advent of the theory of *l'art pour l'art* coincided with the development of aesthetic autonomy as an institution, both in a material sense and in terms of more abstract networks of discourse, which further emphasized the distance between art and life, and it was against this divide that the historical avant-garde reacted by attempting to reconnect them on the basis of a new praxis that refused to acknowledge the inherited forms of art, and that violently rejected the institution "art." For Bürger, this analysis is inscribed in a critical account of what he calls the "neo-avantgarde," i.e. the art of the 1950s and 1960s, which he (following the proposal by Marx in *The 18th Brumaire of Louis Bonaparte*) describes as a "farce" or "parody" that merely repeats the gestures of the initial phase, divesting them of their "tragic" force by enshrining them within a fully developed and institutionalized late modernism, where they no longer have any disruptive power. Bürger's analysis is to some extent reminiscent of Hegel's verdict in the *Lectures on Aesthetics*—the avant-garde, from the point of view of its highest determination (i.e. not to represent religious or philosophical truths, as in Hegel, but to overthrow the institution of art itself), is a "thing of the past"— and what remains is little but a melancholy contemplation of the demise of radical art in a situation characterized by the "limitless availability" of artistic means.[3]

3. Hal Foster has famously argued against Bürger that he hypostatizes

The interpretation proposed here will begin from a different angle: the idea of the historical avant-garde as a *transformation* of art that does not necessarily start out from a reflection on earlier forms, but takes its cues from the impact of technology and social change, as forces that changed the very *terrain* of art, not in the sense of a causal relation, but of a freeing of other possibilities. Unlike the temporal schema of various historicist models, this would be something like the time of the *virtual*, as it has been developed by Gilles Deleuze: a time that unhinges the present and the past from themselves, a temporality that, in John Rajchman's apt phrase, points to "quite small 'virtual futures,' which deviate from things known, inserting the chance of indetermination where there once existed only definite probabilities."[4] Such an approach seeks to pose the ques-

    the historical avant-garde as a unique and absolute moment, whereas the actual history of modernism, Foster suggests, shows that many of the revolutionary breaks in fact became readable as such, as *origins of the present*, only in retrospect, in a form of "deferred action," which can be analyzed in psychoanalytical terms; see Foster, *The Return of the Real* (Cambridge, Mass.: MIT, 1996). However, if Foster's critique emancipates us from one kind of historicism, it leads us to another, namely the kind of infinite analysis, where the question of origin still haunts us, although in a displaced form. To some extent, the perspective that will be adopted here, within which the avant-garde is understood as a transformative event that can only partly be conceived as a negation of earlier artistic morphologies, was already prefigured in the critiques leveled against Bürger from a Marxist activist position, and which often took their cue from Benjamin rather than Adorno. See W. Martin Lüdke (ed.): *"Theorie der Avantgarde": Antworten auf Peter Bürgers Bestimmung von Kunst und bürgerlicher Gesellschaft* (Frankfurt am Main: Suhrkamp, 1976).
4.   John Rajchman, *Constructions* (Cambridge, Mass.: MIT, 1998), 9. Deleuze first develops the theory of virtuality in his analysis of Bergson (*Le Bergsonisme* [Paris: PUF, 1966]), and then draws on the concept throughout all of his books. My use of the term here is inspired by what I see as the general drift of Deleuze's ideas, although I make no claim to capture the manifold ways in which he makes use of it. For a study of this theme in Deleuze, which discusses the background in Bergson and Proust, and its application in Deleuze's books on cinema, see Valentine Moulard-Leonard, *Bergson-Deleuze Encounters: Transcendental Experience and the Thought of the Virtual* (Albany: State University of New York Press, 2008). For a fascinating collection of source documents and criti-

tion of the avant-garde not within a succession of styles, but as the irruption of an outside that cannot be accounted for in terms of a linear succession, which also entails a rethinking of the military and spatial connotations of the term "avant-garde." The territory that opens up is not something pre-existing, but is itself created as a spatial possibility in the act of invention; the space of invention is not regulated in advance, "striated" in the vocabulary of Deleuze and Guattari, but "smooth."

From this vantage point, the implications of the avant-garde as a historical event and as a challenge to philosophical aesthetics cannot be exhausted by a reading that situates it as merely a negative response to the autonomy of the institution "art," instead it should be understood in terms of the possibility of seizing, reconfiguring, and even intensifying *other* movements in society and in thought. The potential of art is precisely one of capturing its own *outside* as an *inside*, and in such a way that the respective values of the inside (the aesthetic) and the outside (that which is acted upon) both change their meaning. The question is not "what is," even less "what was" the avant-garde, but: *what could it become?* As Deleuze would say, the future is not a dimension of the *possible*, where actualization takes place in the likeness of the idea or an already established model, but of the *virtual*, a *becoming* that unsettles the past and the present, and introduces difference.

It is on the basis of this intuition that the following three responses will be situated, each of which attempt in their respective ways to grasp the constellation of technology, art, and politics: Walter Benjamin, Ernst Jünger, and Martin Heidegger. In each of them, the project of "destruction" becomes a way to provide

> cal readings that confronts this theme with phenomenology (containing an unpublished 1904 course by Bergson on the theory of memory, a 1960 course by Deleuze on Bergson, as well as the proceedings from two conferences on Bergson and phenomenology in Prague 2002 and in Paris 2003), see Frederic Worns (ed.): *Annales bergsoniennes: Tome 2, Bergson, Deleuze, la phénoménologie* (Paris: PUF, 2004).

the basis for a different experience in which the subject must be rethought in relation to technology, and where another form of collectivity becomes the agency for a transformed conception of politics. But as we will see, this destruction of aesthetic autonomy also runs the risk, to different degrees and in conflicting ways, of aestheticizing politics.

2. 1. Benjamin and the Technology of Reproduction

Unlike Jünger and Heidegger, Benjamin approaches the idea of technology on the basis of a direct dialogue with the artistic avant-garde, and he attempts to formulate a positive and affirmative relation to technology, especially photography and cinema, which he sees as emancipatory forces that will deliver humanity from its dependence on myth and magic. In many cases, however, he remains deeply divided over this issue: sometimes he suggests that technology is a decisive and irrevocable step forward that will show us that reality is always something constructed, on the other hand he sometimes interprets it as an emptying out of the tradition, which gives his writings a melancholy tone.[5]

This dialectical tension between the old and the new, and the gaps and tensions that exist in all cultural forms that lay claim

---

5. Rainer Rochlitz suggests that we in fact may discern three successive claims about aesthetics in Benjamin: in the first phase, the issue is to restore a primordial power of "naming" that unfolds in dialectic between work and philosophical interpretation (as in the first dissertation, on the concept of art criticism in German Romanticism); in the second, which is the one that will occupy us here, the question is how art can be emancipated from beauty, aura, and cult value; in the third phase (as in the essay on the storyteller, or on some motifs in Baudelaire), Rochlitz suggests that he once more discovers the loss of memory that such an emancipation would entail, and in this sense attains a synthesis of the first two. See Rochlitz, "Drei Ästhetik-Paradigmen bei Benjamin," in Klaus Garber and Ludger Rehm (eds.): *Global Benjamin: Internationaler Walter-Benjamin-Kongress 1992* (Munich: Fink, 1999), vol. 1.

to novelty, constitute the nucleus of Benjamin's interpretation of Baudelaire, as we can see in one of the drafts for the Arcades project, "Paris, Capital of the 19th Century" (1935). Such crevices in the fabric of history are not impasses or voids that would simply derail time, rather they have the capacity to open up a retroactive possibility, which is akin to what we above called a time of the *virtual*, which gives us a distance to the present that otherwise would not be possible; it relays a spark from the past to the future by shattering the monolithic quality of the now. For Benjamin, a philosophical grasp of history does not imply a restoration of a temporal *continuum*, but the exacerbation of the *fracture*, where each moment opens up both toward the archaic dimension and the messianic promise of redemption. The fate of art–which, on the one hand, looks backwards towards the downfall of the solitary creator, on the other hand, struggles to establish a new role in the emerging mass societies–here assumes a paradigmatic function for Benjamin's project of releasing the energy hidden inside this transformation and channel it into social and political purposes.

Seen from the vantage point of tradition, the entry of art into the world of the merchant and of the commodity is a loss of substance and autonomy, but more profoundly, Benjamin suggests, it is a dialectical step toward a *liberation of art from itself*, i.e. a destruction of the aesthetic frame that liberates another capacity, provided that the dialectical puzzle-picture formed by this double determination is read in the right way. This is how Benjamin understands the idea of destruction: an "explosion of historical continuity" that is both the condition of possibility for a genuine "experience" and for a "future construction." It proceeds from the experience of poverty, the disintegration of traditional values that "clears the table" and forces us to behave as constructors, as in the case of artists like Klee, Brecht, and Loos. They all practice the art of "erasure" that clears away the relics of the past, a "destructive living" that only allows for a temporary "housing," but in this also prepares for a new dwelling that is attuned to technology (which, as we will see, is both close to and far from Heidegger's later proposals), and enables a different sensory and bodily relation to the world.

This is how Benjamin reads the clash between art-forms and core-forms that Giedion detected in the development of 19th century architecture: the underlying technical structure that breaks through the crust of tradition points ahead to the task of the engineer, which is to wrest art free from the aesthetic enclosure. A similar argument underlies the essay on the work of art in the age of mechanical reproduction, where the new technical forms are photography and cinema, as well as the essay "The Author as Producer," where Benjamin argues that a truly political literature must take its lead from the mass media, and revolutionize both the forms of production and distribution, the paradigm case of which he sees in the new "factographic" literature pioneered by Sergey Tretyakov.[6]

It is to this future dimension that Benjamin's historical work is oriented, the task being, as he writes in a letter to Horkheimer, to "indicate the precise historical position in the present towards which my historical construction related as if to its vanishing point."[7] But as we have noted, he often seems to decry the loss of experience (*Erfahrung*, which in these contexts is opposed to the

---

6. In this there is an element of tragic irony, and perhaps a certain blindness to current history, since Tretyakov, together with the entire artistic avant-garde, was in the process of being subjected to the strictures of Socialist Realism, which in Tretyakov's case would lead to his execution three years later. However, it is also possible to argue that Benjamin picks the already defunct example of Tretyakov precisely because he wants to counter the influence of Moscow on Leftist art; see Maria Gough, "Paris, Capital of the Soviet Avant-Garde," *October*, vol. 101 (Summer 2002).
7. Letter to Horkheimer, October 16, 1935, in *Gesammelte Schriften*, vol. V/2, 1149.

atomism and shallowness of *Erlebnis*), the instrumentalization of language as a mere vehicle of communication, and the loss of art as a purveyor of metaphysical experiences. Precisely by virtue of this contradiction—which should not be taken as sign of psychological indecisiveness, but *lies in the things themselves*, to speak like Hegel—his work both points ahead, from the beginnings of modernism and the first encounter of art and industrial technology, to the avant-garde phase where their integration seemed to promise a new social order, and looks back to the hidden foundations of, and the inevitable loss entailed by, this process. In this sense his writings are themselves puzzle-pictures that can be read in multiple and contradictory ways.

The key text to Benjamin's futurist mode is the 1935 essay, "Das Kunstwerk im Zeitalter seiner technischen Reproduzierbarkeit," where he presents a systematic view of the relation between technology and art, of the ontology of the art object, of the status of spectatorship, and of how the mode of circulation of aesthetic objects in a high capitalist culture might be transformed. Dressed up in a descriptive, and to some extent prognostic language, the essay can in fact be taken as a manual for perception, teaching us how to navigate in a world that does not yet exist, but which is possible to the extent that we understand the new productive forces in an emancipatory way. These forces, he suggests, ought to have made the kind of aesthetic culture that was brought to completion in late 19th century impossible; nonetheless, a reactionary politics will attempt to reclaim them, and even intensify their grip on contemporary culture.

In the second version of the text, Benjamin attempts a speculative analysis of the origin of both art and technology in magic, as the first and undeveloped form of domination over nature. As distance to nature increases, a moment of "play," but also "interplay" of man and nature appears, both of which will subsist in the subsequent notion of art, which always retains traces of play and domination. This theory of art's origin in magic comes close to Benjamin's views on mimesis as the "originary phenomenon" (in the sense of Goethe's *Urphänomen*) of art, in relation to which ordinary language is only a fallen and secondary version, which is hard to reconcile with the much more instrumental version proposed in the essays from the mid-1930s (and here we can see the extent to which Benjamin's various attitudes towards art and aesthetics do not form a simple chronological sequence).

In the most famous passages, dedicated to the concept of aura, the mimetic and magical origin of art is a dimension that underlies and is preserved in aesthetic art, but is finally overcome in the age of mechanical reproducibility. The "unique phenomenon of distance" (with respect to the object's physical support as well as to the concerns of everyday life) disappears in reproduction, which emphasizes the "exhibition value" and makes the work suitable for mass consumption. Transcendence and mystery loosen their grip on us as the works take on a utilitarian value in the shaping of a communal life.

For Benjamin, this consumption does not entail passivity, but *activity*: the emphasis on the technological aspect (cinema is his main example) encourages the spectator to test what he sees, to retrace and reflect on the production process, it liberates perception from its alleged natural bounds, and in analogy to psychoanalysis, it shows us an "optical unconscious" at work. Space and time are themselves *under construction*, and the new art forms uncover our own participation in this process—not however as transcendental subjects in the sense of neo-Kantianism or phenomenology, but as situated bodies in a historically and technologically determined social field.

Unlike aesthetically enclosed works, such as painting and theatre,[8] the new technological art forms, Benjamin says, arise

8. There is undoubtedly a certain irony here, too, in the fact that Benjamin

immediately out of, and reflect back upon, the urban masses, and in this respect they have a direct political significance. For Benjamin these features do not just make such art forms into highly *efficient* political instruments, which is unquestionable, but in addition—the critical point where his position seems less than clear—turn them into instruments whose very technological structure appears *inherently* progressive. The final famous claim of the text to a large extent depends on this premise: when Benjamin opposes the Fascist aestheticizing of politics, which retrieves the lost aura of art and projects it into politics, to the Communist politicizing of art, which draws the correct conclusion from the downfall of aesthetics and liberates the new artistic productive forces from the obsolete relations of production, the basis of this conclusion seems highly precarious.[9]

Our next example, Ernst Jünger, in fact provides a direct counter-image to Benjamin's optimism in his comments on the use of photography and film as a new kind of political weapon, in a series of texts written slightly before Benjamin's artwork essay. Benjamin's interpretation, full of fantasy projections as it may be,

---

systematically opposes the operations of estrangement and construction in cinema to theater, where we allegedly project ourselves onto the stage as if we were following real events, since the main theoretical tools that he applies to cinema are drawn from Brecht's conception of "epic theater," as can be seen in Benjamin's essays on Brecht, in *Versuche über Brecht*. For a discussion of the various senses of "estrangement," see Steve Giles, "Aesthetic Modernity in *Der Dreigroschenprozess* and the Kunstwerk essay," in Peter Osborne (ed.): *Walter Benjamin: Appropriations* (London: Routledge, 2004).

9. The reading of the phrase "aestheticizing of politics" depends of course on what we mean by "aesthetics." In this context, Benjamin is explicitly referring to the doctrine of *l'art pour l'art*, which he understands as the evacuation of all ethical, cognitive, religious, etc., values. There are indeed other ways to aestheticize politics, for instance those that follow the lead of Kant's third Critique and the problem of judgment, as in the case of Arendt and Lyotard. For a discussion of the various sense of "aestheticizing," see Martin Jay, "'The Aesthetic Ideology' as Ideology: or, What Does It Mean to Aestheticize Politics?," *Cultural Critique*, No. 21 (Spring 1992).

is in fact, as we suggested initially, less a description than a manual for perception: it seeks to release the new art forms from an interpretation that is all too obvious, and it is situated at a historical juncture where the future is not yet decided. Its utopian energy derives from this projective strategy, but also from its blindness to the present. Adorno's oft-quoted critique of the artwork essay clearly pinpoints many of its questionable aspects: the distance of art from society attained in reification is not just something negative, Adorno notes, but the condition for the autonomy that allows art to have a critical purchase on the world, whereas the immediate conversion of reification to use-value turns art into an instrument of manipulation, and in fact may lead to an "inrush of barbarism." Similarly, Benjamin underestimates the disenchantment produced by *artistic* techniques, as in the case of Schönberg's serial method or Mallarmé's poetry, whereas the technical division of labor in cinema in most cases is deployed to attain the most conventional of results. In fact, as Adorno famously claims, mass cultural and autonomous forms of art only exist by virtue of an interplay within which they constitute each other's repressed truths—they are the torn halves of an integral freedom, to which, however, they do not add up, and all attempts to heal this wound risk destroying the very freedom in the name of which they are undertaken.

2. 2. Jünger and the Metaphysics of the Worker

Jünger begins from the same perception of a historical shift as Benjamin, the poverty and loss of values of a world devastated by war, where technology has become the prevalent force. The conclusions he draws are however completely different, both in the sense that his political stance is on the far right, but also in the sense that he, at least during the period on which we will focus here, eradicates all traces of melancholy. Technology will not liberate us, but rather produce a new type of humanity for which freedom and servitude are the same. This is the Worker, a metaphysical Gestalt that subsumes humanity, where individuality is superseded in a collective body. In this process, Jünger suggests, film and photography will indeed be essential means, although not as instruments for reflection and emancipation, but rather for *subjection*; they are part of a new structure of "total media" that demands complete attention. If art first seems to play only a minor role in Jünger's dystopian vision, this is because the avant-garde impulse that fuses life, art, and technology here constitutes a trans-aesthetic, beyond the sphere of judgment (aesthetic, ethical, or cognitive). In the wake of a particular reading of Nietzsche, the destruction of aesthetics in Jünger makes possible a becoming-aesthetic of the world in its totality, and in this sense Jünger's thought undoubtedly constitutes an example of what Benjamin called an aestheticizing of politics.[10] But he also constitutes an example that, by drawing out some of the consequences of Benjamin's view while wholly subverting their political significance, strikes back at the heart of Benjamin's own theory, which indicates the political indeterminacy of these options.

Jünger's views on technology were worked out in a series

10. This is also how Benjamin reacted to Jünger, in his "Theorien des deutschen Faschismus," *Gesammelte Schriften*, vol. III. The text is a review of a collection of texts on the war edited by Jünger in 1930, *Krieg und Krieger* (this anthology is also where Jünger's essay "Die totale Mobilmachung" was first published). For Benjamin the only logical outcome of Jünger's aestheticizing stance was war. On the background of Benjamin's reading, see Ansgar Hillach, "The Aesthetics of Politics: Walter Benjamin's 'Theories of German Fascism,'" *New German Critique*, No. 17 (Spring 1979). But it must also be noted that Benjamin's opposition to Jünger is based on his competitive claims for an even more encompassing revolutionary violence that will be "ten times" more powerful than could ever be imagined by "the habitués of chtonic forces of horror carrying their Klages in their haversacks"; see *GS* III, 249f, and the commentary by Marcus Bullock, "Walter Benjamin and Ernst Jünger: Destructive Affinities," *German Studies Review*, vol. 21, No. 3 (1998).

of texts from the early 1930s,[11] where he presents it as the latest and highest form of a planetary will to power. His writings have an obvious and immediate connection to the political crisis of the Weimar Republic (which indeed is also true in the case of Benjamin and Heidegger), although this will not occupy us here. If seen within the context of the debate on technology, his writings can be understood as part of an avant-garde aesthetic, both in the sense that they imply that the new political order should be understood as an aesthetic one, and that one of its formative influences comes from the experiences of the artistic avant-garde from the two preceding decades.

Drawing on his experiences in the trenches of the first World War,[12] to which he dedicated his first novel from 1920, *In Stahlgewittern*, Jünger diagnoses a shift not only in the techniques of warfare, but in society at large, from an age of individuality to a period dominated by collective forces, of the Gestalt

11. These earlier ideas were fundamentally modified in many of Jünger's later works, where he develops a more "spiritual" and less affirmatively nihilist position, no doubt under the influence of various critiques leveled at his earlier positions. The philosophically most far-reaching and probing of these critical interpretations can be found in Martin Heidegger's essay "Zur Seinsfrage" based on a critical reading of *Der Arbeiter* and Jünger's work from the 1930s. I will return to Heidegger's relation to Jünger in chap. 3 below. For Jünger's later views, which fall outside of the scope of the present discussion (and also must include the work of his brother, Friedrich Georg), see Friedrich Strack (ed.): *Titan Technik: Ernst und Friedrich Georg Jünger über das technische Zeitalter* (Würzburg: Königshausen und Neumann, 2000).

12. Many have chosen to read the more theoretical work as simply an extrapolation of the war trauma, and a way to "fortify" the damaged subject by identifying with a machine-like anonymity. See the discussion of Jünger's literary style in Andreas Huyssen, "Fortifying the Heart—Totally: Ernst Jünger's Armored Texts," *New German Critique*, No. 59 (1993). Huyssen argues somewhat unconvincingly that this disqualifies Jünger from being a modernist writer; against this view, see the more nuanced analysis in Carsten Strathausen, "The Return of the Gaze: Stereoscopic Vision in Jünger and Benjamin," *New German Critique*, No. 80 (2000), who follows the movement in the literary works whereby experiences are lifted up to a third-person level through techniques inspired by photography and cinema.

of the Worker. For Jünger this leads to a new type of "inner experience," whereby the subject is able to understand itself as the origin of this process, and as the paradoxical agent of its own overcoming. The subject finds its place within the "total mobilization" of energy and resources, which is what fundamentally takes place behind the surface conflicts of ideologies during the war: a full deployment of the will to power, where the collective Gestalt of the Worker displaces the Warrior with his individual heroism.

This is the vision presented in the 1932 treatise *Der Arbeiter*, which attempts to survey the historical process from a distance that the author sometimes describes as "lunar." On the one hand it is obviously a text with violent political implications, on the other hand, as Siegfried Kracauer pointed out in his review, the kind of "Gestaltschau" claimed by Jünger is just as much a flight from politics,[13] or a reinterpretation of the course of political events on a metaphysical level. In all sectors of society—economy, law, politics, education, etc.—a collective order breaks forth, where the Worker assumes the place of the individual, although for Jünger, this is not so much a sociologically observable process defined through a set of relations to productive forces and social relations,[14] as the emergence of a form situated beyond the vicissitudes of empirical history. Jünger's interpretation of technology follows a similar mythical trajectory, it is only the outward form of an underlying will to power, which here comes close to what Heidegger would later call the *Ge-Stell*, i.e., the end of metaphysics

13. Kracauer, "Gestaltschau oder Politik," in *Schriften: Aufsätze 1932–1965*, ed. Inka Mülder-Bach (Frankfurt am Main: Suhrkamp, 1990).
14. This does not mean that Jünger simply opposes a Marxist analysis, but rather that he aspires to reach another dimension, as he writes in a letter to his French translator Henri Plard in 1978: "I definitely reject the anti-Marxist interpretation [of *Der Arbeiter*]. Marx fits into the 'worker's system,' but he does not fill it out completely. Something similar could be said about the relation to Hegel." *Sämtliche Werke* (Stuttgart: Klett-Cotta, 1978–1983), vol. 8, 390.

as a pure will to power without other aims than its own increase and solidification as planetary domination (which is why, as we will see later, Heidegger can read Jünger as an anticipation of his own analysis of technology, albeit in a form that remains blind to itself and remains incapable of overcoming nihilism, and instead *enacts* it in its ultimate form).

For Jünger, this transformation of the metaphysical structure of modernity means that it assumes a *total* work character, where man and machine are joined together in the new bond of "organic construction," visible in all aspects of life, from warfare to the new metropolitan landscape that absorbs nature and countryside into one gigantic workspace. Here, art too is called upon to divest itself of its merely aesthetic function and become part of the new "elementary forces" of a transfigured humanity. This emphasis on the new unity can be seen on the one hand as an attempt to retrieve the organic inside the technological, which we also find in expressionist theories of urbanism, on the other hand as an attempt to locate an authentic experience within the fragmentation and mechanization of the body, where it appears as a "mass ornament," and as an *Erlebnis* whose "degree of reality," as Kracauer writes in a famous essay, "is still higher than that of the artistic productions which cultivate obsolete noble sentiments in obsolete forms."[15] In Jünger, this experience of uniformity and loss of individuality is something that must be accounted for, not primarily as loss, but as the entry into a different dimension that must be described as beyond good and evil with respect to the earlier culture that it displaces.

Like Benjamin, Jünger suggests that cinema, photography, and media based on industrial and/or information technology (for instance radio, with its "total entertainment character")

15. Siegfried Kracauer, "The Mass Ornament" (1927), in Kracauer, *The Mass Ornament*, trans. Thomas Y. Levin (Cambridge, Mass.: Harvard University Press, 1995), 79.

will shift the nature of our urban and political space. In his compilations of photographs, *Der gefährliche Augenblick* (1931) and *Die veränderte Welt* (1933), he presents us with a series of images, juxtaposed to brief descriptive and interpretative statements, displaying the industrial world of the Worker, and its effects on time and space, the body, desire, and fantasy. The photograph in particular, he suggests, initiates a new mode of perception, a colder consciousness that inserts a distance between the will and our sensibility, which is an effect of the "the technological order itself, this great mirror in which the increasing objectification of our life appears most clearly, and that in a special way is sealed off from the grip of pain." "Technology," he concludes, "is our uniform."[16]

Unlike Benjamin, who sees the gradual technologization of the life-world as revealing its always already constructed nature, and thus as demanding our active participation, even a kind of expertise that engenders skepticism and reflection, Jünger first emphasizes the moment of domination and passivity, which however is overcome in an ulterior moment of identification, where subjection and freedom become indistinguishable. Here, the emancipatory capacities claimed by Benjamin have been displaced by a conception that tends to oscillate between the demonic (technology as a force that drives the development, outside of human control) and the instrumental (technology as "clothing" of the worker). If nihilism for Benjamin is a positive condition that is overcome by a constructive attitude, for Jünger it can only countered by being introjected in the subject, which thereby identifies with the forces that threaten it.

The third response that will be dealt with here, in Heidegger's analysis of the origin of the work of art, seems at first to unfold in a rather different dimension. Whereas Benjamin and Jünger both

16. "Über den Schmerz," *Sämtliche Werke* vol. 7, 174.

embrace technological modernity, and even want to intensify its capacity for destroying inherited values, for Heidegger modernity seems to be nothing but a loss of the potential of "great art" in a culture permeated by *Erlebnis* and aesthetics. In order to cross-read these three texts, we need, then, to take a step back and say a few words on the horizon within which Heidegger understands the question of the origin of the work of art.

2.3. Heidegger and the Origin of the Work of Art

The response given by Heidegger in *The Origin of the Work of Art* might at first seem wholly at odds with both Benjamin and Jünger. The very orientation of the quest for "great art" appears to reject modernity, and even more so modernism, and instead return us to some archaic fantasy of the time of the ancient Greek temple. Works of the modern period, on the other hand, which are enclosed in aesthetics and art-historical discourse, and have become the object of subjective enjoyment and taste, would seem to be located at the opposite end of the spectrum when compared to the greatness of a work that is able to gather a world around itself, and open up the fundamental strife between concealment and unconcealment out of which our world emerges.

And yet, like many of the proponents of the avant-garde, Heidegger claims that it is only through a destruction of aesthetics that we can approach the *truth* of the work of art, which is not to exist as the object of taste and enjoyment, but to provide the basic outlines of a world. In this, Heidegger's backward gaze at Greece notwithstanding, he may be said to participate in the discourse of modernism and the avant-garde: if the work, as he will suggest, is a "thrust" (*Stoss* or "event," *Ereignis*, as he will say later on) that cannot be anticipated from what precedes it; if it opens a visibility that gives a new phenomenal presence and legibility to everyday objects; if it breaks away from institutionalized reception in itself, creating a space for its preservers—would it then not be possible to say that Heidegger's treatise on the origin of the work of art is quintessentially modernist in the forms of its proposals, even though its preferred references remain in the classicizing canon (although this too, as we will see, is far from the entire truth, as the case of van Gogh will show)?

In order to grasp the context of these claims, we must note that Heidegger's approach to the work of art is itself inscribed in a turn within his own thinking, where he moves away from the project of fundamental ontology and into the history of being, and thought becomes historical in a different sense than in the work from the 1920s. After the turn the task is no longer to found the edifice of traditional metaphysics, but to overcome, deconstruct, and eventually take leave of the project of philosophy as it has been handed down to us from the Greek origin to the present. The discussion on how Heidegger's turn should be interpreted, why the project of fundamental ontology was abandoned, even to what extent there even is such a thing as a turn, is almost infinite, and it of course cannot be reviewed here.[17] For my purposes, it may suffice to note that the encounter with, and the profound need to meditate on the work of art, is one of the essential ways in which this shift takes place. Regardless of how we assess the ramifications of the abandonment of fundamental ontology, it remains true that the earlier work from the 1920s pays little attention to art and aesthetic issues, whereas the references begin to multiply from the 1930 onwards, which is where the turn is normally located. In this sense, I would argue that there is a whole constellation of texts—the lectures on Nietzsche from 1936 onwards (the first being dedicated to "The Will to

---

17. I sketch an interpretation of this in "Heidegger's Turns," in *Essays Lectures*, chap. 3.

Power as Art"), on Hölderlin, beginning with the 1934–35 lectures on *Germanien* and *Der Rhein*, as well as the meditations on Sophocles in *Einführung in die Metaphysik* (1935)—in which the essential aspects of the turn begin to appear, as well as the idea that metaphysics can only be overcome through a *Denken* that approaches, though without identifying with, the movement of *Dichten*. A discussion of this entire constellation cannot be undertaken here, and I will only address the claims put forth in *The Origin of the Work of Art*.

As we have noted, for Heidegger the true significance of art for thinking can only appear if we succeed in overcoming the kind of frame that is imposed by aesthetics, which is what gave the title to the colloquium with Kurt Bauch in the winter of 1935/36, "Die Überwindung der Ästhetik in der Frage nach der Kunst," where many of the ideas were worked out.[18] The concept of *Überwindung* here inserts itself in a long series of terms: repetition (*Wiederholung*), destruction (*Destruktion*), dismantling or deconstruction (*Abbau*), and later also "taking leave of" (*Verwindung*), which all denote a relation to the tradition that has to do with liberating a dormant possibility inside an inherited concept by examining its formation and structure. In this series of terms, there is a certain shift in perspective from the possibility of retrieving a positive content to an emphasis on something "unthought" (*das Ungedachte*) that has *necessarily* remained outside the scope of the history of metaphysics, and which points to one of the crucial questions of how we should understand the turn. In the case of aesthetics, the second view seems to be predominant, and Heidegger does not seek to unearth possibilities inside this concept as it has developed from the 18th century onwards, but instead looks to the idea of "art" for this critical leverage.

18. For the exchanges between Bauch and Heidegger, see Martin Heidegger und Kurt Bauch, *Briefwechsel, 1932–1975*, *Martin Heidegger Briefausgabe* section. II, vol. 1 (Freiburg: Alber, 2010).

For Heidegger, aesthetics as a relation to art seems to be based first on the Platonic distinction between the sensible (*to aistheton*) and the supersensible (*to noeton*), and then, on the Cartesian reinterpretation of this divide within the sphere of subjectivity and the *ego cogito*. An indication of this is that the series of "basic facts" from the history of aesthetics suggested in the 1936 lectures on Nietzsche and the will to power as art, proceeds directly from Descartes to Hegel, and ignores the whole 18th century development, including the very formation of the term aesthetics and the role of Kant.[19] In the postface he points to the element of *Erlebnis* (which for him is the final outcome of the aesthetic tradition) as the "element" in which art dies, and in a marginal note he suggests that true task is to find "a wholly different element for the 'becoming' of art" ("ein ganz anderes Element für das 'Werden' der Kunst zu erlangen").[20]

Heidegger's initial question in *The Origin of the Work of Art* bears on the "essence" of the work of art understood as origin, and here we should connect Heidegger's understanding of *Wesen* to the idea of the "becoming" of art. He is neither asking for a transcendental determination of aesthetic judgment or the judgment of taste, as in Kant's *Critique of Judgment*,[21] nor for the

19. Heidegger, *Nietzsche I* (Pfullingen: Neske, 1961), 94ff. For a systematic discussion of Heidegger's relation to the tradition of aesthetics, see Gerhard Faden, *Der Schein der Kunst: Zu Heideggers Kritik der Ästhetik* (Würzburg: Königshausen und Neuman, 1986). Bearing in mind that the picture presented in the 1936 Nietzsche lectures is extremely sketchy and perhaps serves a polemical purpose, it is nonetheless true that Heidegger never provided us with a more substantial account. A different genealogy of aesthetics, beginning with Baumgarten's rethinking of Rationalism, is surely possible; see for instance Christoph Menke, *Kraft: Ein Grundbegriff ästhetischer Anthropologie* (Frankfurt am Main; Suhrkamp, 2008). I hope to return to this question in the future; here, the historical accuracy of Heidegger's account is not the issue, but rather how the account informs his understanding of the possibilities of art in his own present.
20. *Der Ursprung des Kunstwerkes*, in *Holzwege*, *Gesamtausgabe*, vol. 5, 67, and margin note b.
21. Heidegger only rarely discusses Kant's third Critique, which may

role of art in the historical unfolding of spirit and reason, as in Hegel's *Lectures on Aesthetics*, although the proximity to Hegel's historical question remains a problem, to which Heidegger returns at the end of the text. The origin of art here means the "provenance of its essence" (*Herkunft ihres Wesens*): essence is

> indicate that he sees it as irrevocably entangled in subjectivity and a theory of taste. At one point in *Nietzsche I* he however makes a surprising connection between Nietzsche and Kant. The context is a discussion of "intoxication" and "rapture" (*Rausch*) in Nietzsche, where Heidegger suggests that this rapture is not primarily a subjective and undetermined going-beyond, a mere projection, but always related to *forms*, which are autonomous in relation to the movement of going beyond. These forms are the condition of rapture, and not the other way around. In a brief digression he also defends Kant's notion of beauty as disinterested against Nietzsche's attacks, and proceeds to link their respective conceptions by construing disinterestedness, or the "freie Gunst" as Kant also calls it, as a "Seinlassen," and rhetorically asks whether it is not to be understood, in opposition to Nietzsche's hasty dismissal, as the "highest effort of our existence, the liberation of our self toward the setting free of that which has a dignity in itself, so that it may have it in a pure way" ("die höchste Anstrengung unseres Wesens, die Befreiung unseres Selbst zur Freigabe dessen, was in sich eine eigene Würde hat, damit es sie rein nur habe" (*Nietzsche I*, 129). As an interpretation of Kant this is of course highly questionable, and Heidegger does not give any further support for this reading, whose function within the overall argument at this point seems to be a protection of Nietzsche, to a *certain extent*, from the charge of subjectivism: when Nietzsche speaks of the interest and pleasure involved in aesthetic experience, and of how it affects us in the innermost core of our being, he is, without being aware of it, returning to what is at least *here* understood by Heidegger to be the basic tenet of Kant's philosophy of art. This is however an aside, and the third Critique quickly vanishes from sight. Henri Declève, in his systematic study of Heidegger's various references to Kant throughout his work, concludes that the extensive and negative reading of the transcendental motif after the *Kehre* "ne laisse guère de place, il faut le reconnaître, à cette nouvelle lecture." (*Heidegger et Kant* [The Hague: Nijhoff, 1970], 229). Jeffrey Maitland provides a reconstructed positive Heideggerian reading of the third Critique, where he follows the lead of Heidegger's brief remark in *Nietzsche I* cited above, in "An Ontology of Appreciation: Kant's Aesthetics and the Problem of Metaphysics," in *The Journal of the British Society for Phenomenology*, vol. 13, No. 1 (1982). He concludes that "Kant's disinterested appreciation is structurally the same as Heidegger's poetic dwelling" (60), and that it is "capable of revealing by participating in the belonging together of thinking and Being, the source of the true, the good and the beautiful as the Same" (67).

not an abstract generality, a *quidditas*, but a coming-to-presence in a temporal movement that is an essential part of being's historical unfolding. This is a movement which also establishes the "truth" within which a particular world becomes legible, and in this sense it cannot be reduced to a mere object of a subjective enjoyment rooted in a sensible apprehension of particulars. The latter is in fact a view shared by both Kant and Hegel, although the ultimate end of this process is different: for Kant it is the establishing of a para-conceptual harmony that unites reason and sensibility, for Hegel the sublation (*Aufhebung*) of particulars into the universalizing grasp of reason, which is why art, structurally (within the *Encyclopedia*) as well as historically (in spirit's movement from Greece to modernity), for him becomes a "thing of the past" (*ein Vergangenes*).[22]

Heidegger takes us through a series of determinations of the work that takes its starting point in the idea of a thing, to which something would be added (aesthetic value, certain perceptive qualities, etc.), which can be found in various neo-Kantian theories, but also in certain strands of phenomenological aesthetics that were being worked out in the wake of Husserl.[23] For Heidegger all

22. Hegel's famous claim in the Introduction to the Lectures, that art "in all these respects, considered in its highest vocation, is and remains for us a thing of the past" (*Vorlesungen über die Ästhetik*, in *Werke*, eds. Eva Moldenhauer and Karl Markus Michel [Frankfurt am Main: Suhrkamp, 1986], vol. 13, 25), seems on the one hand to testify to a kind of anti-modern stance—art existed once, or to the fullest extent, only in Greece, but cannot be essential in modernity—although it can just as well be interpreted in the opposite fashion: it is only when art is emancipated from the task of presenting the absolute that it can assume its proper aesthetic role, and become a truly autonomous form of experience in relation to philosophy and religion. Both of these readings would however place Hegel in opposition to Heidegger, and the second, which is the one favored in most contemporary readings, even more so, since Heidegger can be understood as attempting to retrieve the kind of unity that Hegel saw as inevitably lost.
23. Gadamer points to the aesthetic theory of Nicolai Hartmann; see "Einleitung," in Martin Heidegger, *Der Ursprung des Kunstwerkes* (Stuttgart: Reclam, 1960). Following Husserl, beginning already around the time of

of these theories miss both the thinghood of the thing and the workhood of the work, whose relation must be understood in a different fashion: it is not on the basis of the thing that we may understand the artistic as something "added," nor can we take our cues from equipment (*Zeug*) and simply strip it of its utility, but it is when starting from the work that we can situate both the thing and equipment.

Particularly important here is the relation to equipment.

> the transcendental turn of phenomenology announced in 1913 in the first volume of *Ideas*, there was also a series of attempts to work out the a priori or eidetic conditions of the aesthetic object. In 1927 Werner Ziegenfuss could look back on this development and publish a thesis dedicated to a systematic survey of works written from a more or less phenomenological standpoint, which all in various ways dealt with what in Husserl's vocabulary could be called the "regional ontology" of the work of art; see Werner Ziegenfuss, *Die phänomenologische Ästhetik* (Berlin: Arthur Collignon, 1928). The early history of phenomenological aesthetics is still relatively unexplored; for two works that survey this development, see Gabriele Scaramuzza, *Le origini dell'estetica fenomenologica* (Padua: Antenore, 1976), and Georg Bensch, *Vom Kunstwerk zum ästhetischen Objekt: Zur Geschichte der phänomenologischen Ästhetik* (Munich: Fink, 1994). Roman Ingarden's later investigations into the layers of signification in the literary work of art (*Das literarische Kunstwerk*, 1931) constitute a landmark in this development, and it was continued after the war in Mikel Dufrenne's systematic analyses of aesthetic experience (*Phénoménologie de l'expérience esthétique*, 1953). Heidegger's questions in *The Origin* can be read as a direct counter-move to this tendency, and his rejection of the concept of aesthetics implies that the "event" of the work demands of thought that it should rethink its own concepts, and aspires eventually to transform the discourse of philosophy itself. Furthermore, that this was a historical *repetition* of the question, was within the first type of phenomenological theory largely unconscious, or a least not a thematic focus, whereas for Heidegger it would take us back not only to idealism, but even, as if in a series of ever-widening circles, to Plato and a certain restaging of the "ancient quarrel," the *palaia diaphora*, in the *Republic*, where poetry appears as the *rival* par excellence of philosophy. Husserl in fact, at a very crucial juncture in his career, suggested a parallel between the phenomenological *epoche* and the aesthetic attitude, although this proximity seems never to have become a decisive issue for him, and it never lead him to any in-depth questioning of the primacy of the theoretical attitude. For a discussion of Husserl's views, as they are laid out in the famous letter to Hofmannsthal from 1907, and in the *Husserliana* volume on *Phantasie, Bildbewusstsein, Erinnerung*, see my "Phenomenology and the Possibility of a Pure Art: Husserl's Letter to Hofmannsthal," in *Site* 26–27 (2009).

First of all, Heidegger claims, it has served as the basis for the traditional form-matter pair, which has informed all art theory and aesthetics, eventually congealing into a "conceptual machinery that nothing is capable of withstanding," and which must be resisted, or more precisely, brought back to its own origin; second, the analysis of equipmentality implicitly presented here points to a shift inside Heidegger's own work from *Being and Time* onward,[24] which has consequences for how we understand the turn; and third, it is by way of this somewhat inconclusive and interrupted meditation on equipmentality that we are presented with the idea of the work of art as the "putting-into-work" (*ins-Werk-Setzen*) of the truth of beings, which is pivotal for the whole essay.

The disclosure of the truth of equipment famously occurs through the meditative encounter with van Gogh's painting of a pair of peasant shoes,[25] which has the function more of an

24. Readers of Heidegger are divided on this point. The first to stress that the position of the tool here undergoes an important shift was Otto Pöggeler, *Der Denkweg Martin Heideggers* (Pfullingen: Neske, 1963). Contrary to this, both Friedrich-Wilhelm von Herrmann, *Heideggers Philosophie der Kunst* (Frankfurt am Main: Klostermann, 1980), and Joseph J. Kocklemans, *Heidegger on Art and Art Works* (Dordrecht: Nijhoff, 1985) emphasize the continuity with *Being and Time*, as well as the recent commentary by Karsten Harries, *Art Matters* (Dordrecht: Springer, 2009) who suggests that Heidegger here "follows, at least provisionally, this clue provided by *Being and Time*" (80). I would here prefer to side with Hubert Dreyfus, who has pointed to a long-term fundamental displacement of the tool, from *Being and Time* where it is always directed back to *Dasein* as the final for-the-sake-of-which (*Worumwillen*), and where the whole of nature is potentially part of the "Zeugganzheit," to the last texts, where the new conception of thing and world displaces the final for-the-sake-of-which to the play of the world. The interesting effect of Dreyfus's analysis is, as he himself notes, that it inscribes *Being and Time* in the unfolding of modern technicity. See Hubert Dreyfus, "De l'ustensilité à la techne: le statut ambigu de l'ustensilité dans l'Etre et le Temps," in Michel Haar (ed.): *Heidegger* (Paris: Cahiers de L'Herne, 1983). The view in *Being and Time* may be taken as "functionalist" view of nature, as I suggest in "Heidegger's Turns," in *Essays, Lectures*, 105f.
25. For a further discussion of Heidegger's identification of the painting and its motif, which has caused long and inconclusive controversies, see

epiphany than of a phenomenological fantasy variation leading us toward an *eidos*,[26] and also provides us with the first access to the conceptual pair "earth" and "world" (which implicitly becomes the origin of the distinction between matter and form). Truth, *aletheia* as disclosure and openness, is what happens through the work, and it can no longer be exclusively brought back into the existential structure of *Dasein*, just as the emphasis on the withdrawal and unconcealment of earth shifts the valence of the earlier analyses of the worldliness of the world.

This truth, however, only occurs to the extent that the work takes an essential part in *founding* it, which seems precluded in the world of aesthetics, taste, and institutionalized reception. This appears however to be at odds with the example of van Gogh's painting, which already points to the whole question of the possibility of an authentically *modern* work of art for Heidegger: the painting shows us the truth of equipment, and yet it cannot be said to act in the same instituting and world-constitutive fashion as "great art" in the full sense of the term.

As a counter-image to the modern work, Heidegger then presents us with the authority of the Greek temple, which here has

Karsten Harries, *Art Matters*, 84ff.
26. The idea of phenomenological variation underlies Kocklemans's defense of Heidegger's art-historical errors, when he says that the painting is only a "starting point of the description, which, as phenomenological description, has to reach far beyond the actual starting point, which itself merely prepares a 'categorial intuition'" (*Heidegger on Art and Art Works*, 126), which in this case would relate to the essential character of equipment. And yet, as Kocklemans himself notes, the point of the whole passage is not to elucidate the being of *equipment* as such; through this elucidation, which nevertheless remains a *detour*, Heidegger searches for a new access to the work of art as the happening of truth. *The painting itself has spoken*, Heidegger emphatically claims, it has transposed us "elsewhere," into the domain of *aletheia*, and it did not serve as merely the starting point for an eidetic variation bearing on the essence of equipment (there is no discussion of various forms of equipment, no counter-examples are presented and no variation is being carried out; what we are presented with, is more a kind of enacted *parousia* of truth, rhetorically initiated by the "dennoch" which opens up the description).

the function of ascertaining the *origin*; it does nor depict anything, but gathers a world around itself, it allows the earth to presence as the obverse side of unconcealment, and organizes a social, political, and religious space. In doing this it allows the "originary strife" (*Urstreit*) between concealment and unconcealment, which as such lies *before* the event of the work, to presence as a "cut" or "rift" (*Riß*), which first occurs between earth and world, and then acquires contour and shape (*Umriß*) in the work. In this sense we can see how that which on the level of traditional aesthetics appears as a difference between form and matter is only a reflection of this more profound rift between earth and world. We must here also note that the opening of a world is not solely ascribed to the work of art, but also to the "act that founds a political state," to the "nearness to that which is not simply a being, but the being that is most in being," to the "essential sacrifice," and to the "questioning of the thinker." The relation between these instituting and founding operations will remain obscure throughout the text, although the idea of a *work* seems to privilege the occurring of truth that belongs to art: the "impulse towards the work" (*Zug zum Werk*) that is materialized in the temple appears to be the model for the other events of truth, which indicate the extent to which this understanding of the artwork too partakes in an "aestheticizing" conception of politics, although it is made possible precisely by the destruction of what is traditionally understood by aesthetics.

The choice of architecture as the paradigmatic case is significant, and Heidegger here implicitly takes up a dialog with Hegel. For Hegel, architecture is that which *recedes* in Greece in order to allow the universality of Man to appear in the form of the freestanding sculpture,[27] whereas Heidegger stresses the opacity and

27. For a further discussion Hegel's theory of architecture as the art of ground and materiality, see my "Hegel and the Grounding of Architecture," in Michael Asgaard and Henrik Oxvig (eds.): *The Paradoxes of Appearing: Essays on Art, Architecture, and Philosophy* (Baden: Lars Müller

concealment whereby architecture connects to the earth, but also transforms it into a "native soil" for a certain people. In this it can acquire a universal significance only in a secondary fashion, and the history whose ground it forms ("Art is history in the essential sense that it grounds history," Heidegger says) remains a particular history.

A similar structure underlies the analysis of the afterlife of the work, where it is entrusted to the "preservers." The instituting event, which Heidegger describes as the unity of a bestowing, a grounding, and a beginning, involves first a thrust that releases us from the past as an address to the future preservers, a "historical human collective" whose ground is the earth revealed by the work. As this grounding, it also draws from a source located beyond any individual genius, and is essentially tied to a historical people. The third dimension, beginning, finally connects past and future; it has already reached ahead to the farthest future, and connects the first and the last in a circular movement, although this circle (whose proximity to its Hegelian counterpart is never addressed) remains concealed to us.

This instituting Heidegger calls poesy (*Dichtung*), which has the function of grounding "beings as a whole, as beings themselves"—and which once more seems essentially bound up with the Greek moment: "This foundation happened for the first time in Greece," Heidegger states. But does this mean that we have to remain within the space opened by Greek art? If Greece was the *first* site for art and philosophy's irruption into a finite historical world, does it also remain the measure for everything that is to come? On the one hand, Heidegger seems to acknowledge that different epochs have their respective horizons and modes of openness, and provide a "thrust" that sets history on a new track; on the other hand

Publishers, 2009). The example of architecture is extremely important for Heidegger's understanding of the essence of technology, as we will see in the following chapter.

the "shapes" produced by art are dependent on the original sending, the *Geschick* of openness, which is fundamentally Greek.

What, then, about modernity, not to speak of post-modernity (to the extent that we trust such a distinction)? Does the instituting gesture, which reaches all the way into the future, require that art must, in order to remain art, preserve a link to the origin, to Greece as the true *Anfang* that will always remain ahead of us? Heidegger's position may be taken as a case of a belated traditionalism, whose roots would take us back to German Idealism. But we must also bear in mind that for Heidegger, Greek philosophy was itself marked by the retreat of being and the ontological difference, by an "un-thought" that does not allow for any simple return. The history of being can be understood as *one* only on the basis of the Greek moment, but this unity is itself founded on a forgetting that can never be undone, only accepted as a loss, the *lethe* of *a-letheia* that belongs to being itself.

But this seemingly Greco-centric figure of thought cannot be sufficient, when Heidegger concludes that the question concerning the essence of art was not a question of Greece, that it in fact was not a historiographical question at all, but resulted from a contemporary need. What the question bears on is whether art once more can become an origin in the sense established above, or whether Hegel's judgment on the end of art in modernity still holds. This seems at first to position the question of modern art as an insurmountable aporia: it must either return to the Greek origin, which is impossible—the world of the temple has crumbled, the flight of the Gods is irrevocable—or assume its modern destiny, which seems to be a state of melancholy, a work of mourning in relation to the past. Heidegger's question of the origin of the work of art thus leaves the question suspended: to the extent that it is backward looking, there can be no "great art" in modernity; to the extent that it partakes of a modernist sensibility, it must end with a question mark.

2.4. Destruction and Beyond

In the introduction to this second part, the idea of a destruction of aesthetics was presented as the task of the avant-garde. On the one hand, this destructive move appears as a kind of nihilism, by dint of its clearing away of the inherited values of art and culture; on the other hand it is a response to the technological transformations of the life-world that seeks to restore a certain power to art, and that can take the downfall of the traditional work as its point of departure, but also the new social forces that make a different collective possible, where aesthetics and politics form a new and unstable alloy.

A common ground for an interpretation of the three philosophical diagnoses discussed above would thus be the question of *nihilism*: each of them defines, undoubtedly in ways that are mutually conflictual and do not lend themselves to any simple synthesis, a situation characterized by the downfall of inherited values, and the possibility of passage "beyond the line" (to use the figure that organizes the later debate between Jünger and Heidegger, to which we will return in the next section), the zero point, or *nihil* of tradition. In Benjamin's liquidation of the tradition that emancipates new forces of artistic production for which a radical poverty is a starting point, in Jünger's Worker and the organic construction that heralds a domination of the planet beyond the demise of 19th century liberalism and individualism, and in Heidegger's attempts to retrieve a different element for the becoming of art, we may discern different attempts to overcome nihilism. For Benjamin and Jünger this overcoming occurs through an identification with what we could call the emergent instead of the residual in technology, which attempts to extract a positive dimension, an inescapable truth, from the reification of consciousness and experience.

The case of Heidegger is, as we have seen, more complicated. *The Origin of the Work of Art* is often read as an anti-modern treatise that denies any possibility of there being great art in modernity. Heidegger's plans to write a sequel to the first text after the war were never realized, and in some interpretations this implies that his philosophical outlook precluded any positive analysis of the specificity of modern art.[28] And indeed, even though the painting by van Gogh plays a crucial role in the organization of the text—it is the example that introduces the idea of art as the setting-into-work of truth, and provides us with a first glimpse of the earth-world complex—it does not yet present us with the full-fledged version of art as the setting-into-work of truth, which only occurs with the Greek temple. The handwritten additional notes (added after the war; a more precise dating remains uncertain) seem to further warrant this conclusion: they speak of the "technological" in the "urge to create," and the emptiness of informal art. In this sense, the case of van Gogh's painting points to a *problem* in modern art, its *insecure* relation to "truth" and "greatness," and neither excludes nor affirms its capacity. The final verdict on Hegel's judgment, Heidegger says at the end, has not fallen, and his meditation has the purpose of re-opening the proceedings.

The interpretation presented in the following sections intends to develop this perspective. On the basis of Heidegger's later texts, I contend that his analysis of the essence of technology in fact provides the grounds for an understanding of modern art that shows it to be not only a necessary counterpart to technology, but also a way to enter into its essence, to think through it, and attain a free relation to it—a movement pointed out in the essay "The Question Concerning Technology": "Because the essence of technology is nothing technological, essential

---

28. Otto Pöggeler, *Philosophie und Politik bei Heidegger* (Freiburg: Alber, 1972), 157. In a later work, *Bild und Technik* (Munich: Fink, 2002), Pöggeler returns to this question in a much more detailed interpretation, drawing especially on Heidegger's notes on Klee.

reflection upon technology and decisive confrontation with it must happen in a realm that is, on the one hand, akin to the essence of technology and, on the other, fundamentally different from it. *Such a realm is art.*" The truth of modern art—truth in the sense of *aletheia*, i.e. the twofold movement of opening up a world of sense and of withdrawing its foundation—would in this sense be the undoing of all traditional forms of beauty, and what is "great" about modern art would be the way in which it tears apart any stable idea of a "native soil" and prepares us for a way to think this soil, the ground, the collective and the historical being-together as an unfinished, open, and even "nameless" possibility, as will be the case in Heidegger's late reflections on the spatiality of sculpture.

The later texts are in this sense to be taken as a dismantling, in the sense of an *ab-bauende* operation that liberates a dormant potential. In *The Origin*, the question of technology is not addressed as such, although other texts from the same period, notably the discussion of Sophocles' *Antigone* in *Einführung in die Metaphysik*, associate the concept with power or violence (*Gewalt*),[29] which however always remain impotent in the face of the overpowering presence of *physis*. It is precisely this violent understanding of *techne* that will be considerably subdued in the later writings.

For the later Heidegger, it is only by excavating the unity of art and technology in the Greek *techne* that we may prepare for

29. For a discussion of this theme, see Daniel Payot, *Le statue de Heidegger* (Paris: Circé, 1998); Michael Gelvin, "Heidegger and Tragedy," in William Spanos (ed.): *Martin Heidegger and the Question of Literature* (Bloomington: Indiana University Press, 1979); Clare Pearson Geiman "Heidegger's Antigones," in Richard Polt and Gregory Fried (eds.): *A Companion to Heidegger's Introduction to Metaphysics* (New Haven and London: Yale University Press, 2001). For an extended discussion of violence and power in Heidegger and Benjamin, see Stefan Knoche, *Benjamin – Heidegger: Über Gewalt; Die Politisierung der Kunst* (Vienna: Turia + Kant, 2000).

a new and free relation to technology, which does not imply a return, but rather an answer to the question posed at the end of *The Origin*, whether great art is possible in the modern world. This, then, does not at all amount to any wholesale rejection of modernity—as we will see, it may even, if read in a certain way, constitute the most ruthless acknowledgement of our condition of no return. In the following sections I will trace this line of thought, as it cuts across Heidegger's texts and connects them to the question of modern art, which is a way to perform, in relation to his work, the *Aus-einander-Setzung* that he himself proposed in relation to Nietzsche; to think through him, beyond, and against him, in order to come back to him differently.[30]

In relation to Benjamin, Heidegger's analyses in the mid-1930s may appear simply as a way to restore the aura of the work of art in an age where it seemed to be threatened precisely by the forces of technology.[31] But Heidegger by no means wants to resuscitate concepts like "sense," "value," "culture," or any similar nostalgic figures of thought. The authority of the work that he locates in the Greek model is situated outside of the sphere of aesthetic values, judgments, and taste, and has an ontological function that allows it to found history. The difference is that for Benjamin, the power of the work cannot be to *found* history; rather it en-

30. See Heidegger's introductory methodological remarks in *Nietzsche I*, 13f. This *Aus-einander-Setzung,* literally a "setting apart," should be related to the themes of *Destruktion* and *Abbau*, and instead of a mere confrontation in the sense of a traditional criticism in search of contradictions and inconsistencies in the other thinker's discourse, the setting-apart discerns the different layers of the tradition that are sedimented in the texts so as to display them in their non-synchronicity, in an attempt to emancipate a possibility for thinking.
31. The identification of Benjamin's aura with Heidegger's *aletheia* proposed by Christopher P. Long, "Art's Fateful Hour: Benjamin, Heidegger, Art and Politics," in *New German Critique*, No. 83 (2001), seems less convincing. In my reading, the aura is what provides the work with a distance towards the world of everyday practices in which it does not partake, whereas *aletheia* for Heidegger is the opening of a world of words, things, and practices that makes them useful and accessible to us.

courages us, by showing the world to be an ongoing construction, even on the level of our experience of space and time, body, and visuality, to take part in the process of formation. The event of the work of art in Heidegger is located beyond the space of social praxis, whereas Benjamin wants to locate it inside these practices, as a way to make us reflect on them.

In order to gauge the differences and similarities, it is however important to locate that particular level where there is a philosophically fruitful exchange going on between them, which lies before the more visible level where they have crystallized into what looks like easily recognizable ideological figures (Heidegger the conservative and Benjamin the radical thinker). The first encounter lies in the fact that for neither one of them can art be construed as a reactive force that would *preserve* a dimension that technology threatens, since that which is to be preserved, for instance a more profound experience, belongs to the aesthetic sphere that must be superseded. Both of them see this aesthetic enclosure as an impediment to the *work* of the work, which is to give form to our practices and social relations, and they also identify its institutional and material support, for instance the museum and other analogous institutions, where works become the object of taste and/or historical learning.

For Heidegger, both in the 1930s and in the later work, Benjamin's emphatic affirmation of technologies of reproduction would be clearly insufficient, since it does not seek the essence of technology, which for Heidegger does not lie in any particular form of technology. This does not imply that Benjamin's answer is simply progressive, in its affirmative view of technology, whereas Heidegger in the 1930s would retreat to a reactionary position that merely seeks to reinstate the aura and the quasi-religious dimension of the work of art. Both of them in fact see the dimension of the holy and sacred in art as essentially a thing of the past: for Heidegger this connection is at the center of the Greek world, whereas Benjamin locates it in the Christian model of contemplation, and at least Benjamin explicitly claims the aesthetic attitude to be a direct descendant of this (the aesthete as a latter-day monk, meditating over a relic that contains the secret message from a mysterious Other, God or the Artist). Aesthetics severs art from its relation to the world, but whereas Heidegger has nothing to say about how such a relation could be restored (above all since he doubts whether it is at all possible), Benjamin's analysis of the new modes of reproduction suggests that new technologies display an almost immediate capacity to organize a new collectivity. For Heidegger, this would simply mean to give in to technology without paying heed to its essence, to which Benjamin would reply that any thought of this essence also has to pass through a direct confrontation with the most sophisticated of our current technologies in their materiality, if it is not to remain abstract and powerless. In this way, their respective reflections provide correctives to each other, while also cautioning us that truth is not to be attained by simply adding them to each other, or juxtaposing them, but by working through their conflictual positions as one of the aporias opened up by the destruction of aesthetics.

Finally, there are the claims of Jünger, who appears to move into a different dimension with his analysis of the Worker. As we have seen, he shares many assumptions with Heidegger, although Heidegger's later attempt to think the essence of technology can be understood as a way to resist the affirmative nihilism of the Worker, and to unearth a philosophical genealogy that remains hidden to Jünger, who in Heidegger's perspective remains caught in a nihilist affirmation of the powers of the present. The difference between Jünger and Benjamin are more striking and obvious, and as we saw, Benjamin himself pointed to Jünger as a paradigm case of the aestheticizing of politics. And yet it can also be argued that Jünger brings out the violence and will to power latent in both Heidegger and Benjamin, the reversibility latent in a straightforward opposition between aestheticizing of politics and politicizing of art.

In view of these contorted exchanges, which bring out the political indeterminacy and capacity for sudden reversal of these avant-gardist proposals, Heidegger's rethinking of technology in the postwar period, which will be the subject of the following chapter, can be understood as a step back from the position of *The Origin of the Work of Art*, a step designed to release the unthought of the earlier work, and in this stepping back, he will once more encounter Jünger, and also—though less directly—Benjamin.

3. The Essence of Technology

3.1. The Essence of Technology

The question of whether Heidegger, in some nostalgic fashion, only points back to a lost Greek source, or whether his meditations in *The Origin of the Work of Art* have the capacity to disclose essential features of the modern work of art, proved to be much more complex than is usually assumed: there is an unmistakable avant-garde attitude in Heidegger, while his main examples (though by no means all, as was shown by the strategic importance of van Gogh) seem to partake of a classicizing tendency. In the following sections I will attempt to resituate the question of art within Heidegger's later work on the essence of technology, elements of which were being worked out already in the 1930s (particularly with respect to Jünger), but which substantially belongs to the postwar period.[1]

Just as little as the earlier discussions on the "essential provenance" of art does Heidegger's discussion of technology engage in any empirical analyses of industrial production, applied sci-

---

1. For general overviews of the emergence and place of the question of technology in Heidegger, see John Loscerbo, *Being and Technology: A Study in the Philosophy of Martin Heidegger* (The Hague: Nijhoff, 1981); Till Platte, *Die Konstellation des Übergangs: Technik und Würde bei Heidegger* (Berlin: Duncker und Humblot, 2004); Hans Ruin, "Ge-stell: Enframing as the Essence of Technology," in Bret W. Davis (ed.): *Martin Heidegger: Key Concepts* (Durham: Acumen, 2010). For a detailed analysis of "Die Frage nach der Technik," see Richard Rojcewicz, *The Gods and Technology: A Reading of Heidegger* (Albany: SUNY Press, 2006) (on technology and art, see 185–212).

ence, machines or technical facilities; it is rather directed toward what he calls its *essence*—a question that will once more lead us close to the question of art. Technology, he says, must be understood as belonging to the "sending of being" (*Geschick des Seins*), and as such it is a mode of disclosure of beings, i.e. a condition for all forms of instrumentality and technicity, which move within a space of the already disclosed. Seen in this perspective, modern technology appears as the last descendant of the Greek *techne*, and as belonging to the sphere of *aletheia*, although in a form that has been radically transformed into a positioning and ordering activity, which Heidegger characterizes by the term "enframing" (*Ge-Stell*). The prefix "Ge-" here indicates the gathering and totalizing power, which draws everything into a cycle of production and transformation, so that the whole of being appears as a "standing reserve" (*Bestand*), or as raw matter for production (which, like *techne*, has its roots in a Greek term, *poiesis*, which in turn finds a distant echo in our modern "poetry").

Re-establishing a link to the Greek *techne* as a different although related mode of disclosure is also what allows Heidegger to connect this discussion to art. In *techne*, art and technology once formed a unity, which today has been lost in a world that has distributed them in two different systems, and even made them into opposed terms: aesthetics takes care of emotional, experiential, and what we could call "soft" concerns, whereas technology is science and rationality materialized, and forms the "hard core" of modern culture, often in opposition to the humanities. It is only if we understand that art and technology together constitute a "constellation of truth," Heidegger suggests, that they can be brought into a new unity that will allow us to see that the question concerning technology is also the question concerning art.

The normal understanding of technology as tools and instrumentality (which is basically the analysis proposed in *Being and Time* in terms of equipmentality) is not false, Heidegger claims, it is even "correct" (*richtig*), although not true (*wahr*): just like the correspondence theory of truth, it shows us how objects appear to a consciousness or a subject, but misses the preceding openness (truth as *aletheia*, disclosure) within which such relations may be set up, and *it is this very openness* which has been transformed within modernity and the gradual unfolding of enframing. In this sense Heidegger does not engage in a critique of instrumental reason, as is often assumed (and just as often in order to dismiss his analyses as one-sided and too totalizing), but attempts to provide an analysis of a dimension that instrumentality already presupposes.

The essence of technology does not lie in any particular function, use, or application, but in a certain way of disclosing entities. This is valid for the Greek *techne* too, and in order to provide a counterpoint to the present, but also to show the fundamental kinship between the two moments, located at the beginning and the end of the history of metaphysics respectively, Heidegger presents us with a reading of Aristotle's theory of causality. In the Greek conception, the *causa finalis* is what gathers the other moments (*causa materialis, formalis*, and *efficiens*) together, whereas modernity has come to focus exclusively on the efficient mode. For the Greeks, Heidegger suggests, bringing forth is not production in the sense of making, but a gathering together in a movement of letting-appear, *apophainesthai*, which straddles the divide between activity and passivity.

In the Greek conception of bringing-forth, *poiesis*, we find not only the nucleus of what will later become separated as art and technology, but also a reference to *physis* as that which emerges and presences out of itself, and into which all modes of letting-appear are inscribed. *Physis*, in the Greek sense that Heidegger wants to retrieve, is never a passive raw material, an inert matter upon which productive acts endowed with efficient causality are exerted, instead that which Aristotle's analysis separates as *hyle* and *morphe* are like the two sides of one process of emergence, which binds the movement of *physis* to the disclosure of *aletheia*. To bring about is to let appear, and the emphasis lies on a "collaborative" dimension rather than on the actions of a subject (all of which can also be found in the Aristotelian analysis of the relation between *physis* and *mimesis* in the *Physics*, to which Heidegger strangely enough does not refer, although it would further support his claim).[2] It is *within* this disclosure that instrumentality can be located, but it can never exhaust it.

Modern technology is still a mode of disclosure, although no longer in the sense of a collaborative *poiesis*, but of a posing and imposing that demands of nature that it provide raw material and energy that can be stored, transmitted, and circulated in a loop that ultimately can be theorized as "securing" and "steering" in the sense of cybernetics, which often seems to be what Heidegger's analysis of technology is pointing to.[3]

2. In *Physics* B II Aristotle proposes two versions of this link, which throughout its many variations has never ceased to impose itself. It is true that all "art imitates nature" (*techne mimetai ten physin*, 194a 23), but then one must also add that "art appears to complete and bring to its end (*epitelei*) that which nature in general is incapable of achieving (*adynatei apergasasthai*) and in another sense it imitates" (199a 15–16). Man's *techne* imitates nature, but in this imitation it also gives something back to nature that nature itself lacks, that without which it would not be fully itself, which underlines what I above called the "collaborative" aspect.

3. Cybernetics was first formulated in the late 1940s in the writings of Norbert Weiner, and sometimes Heidegger explicitly sees it as that which will eventually engulf the philosophical tradition: "Philosophy becomes superfluous," and "the end of philosophy is characterized by the dissolution of its disciplines into autonomous sciences, whose new unification is being achieved in cybernetics." *Zur Frage nach der Bestimmung des Denkens* (St. Gallen: Erker Verlag, 1984), 8. See also the statement in *Denkerfahrungen, 1910–1976* (Frankfurt am Main: Klostermann, 1983), where Heidegger suggests that "in the cybernetically represented world, the difference between automatic machines and living things disappears. It becomes neutralized by the undifferentiated process of information.

Heidegger famously cites the example of the river Rhine, where the power plant is no longer built into the stream like the old wooden bridge, on the contrary the stream is now "built into" (*verbaut in*) the power plant. Here even the sense of "object" disappears, there is no more *Gegenstand* that stands over against us, which is why a critique of the objectification of nature (to which Heidegger is often assimilated) is insufficient; as we have noted earlier, this is what makes possible the "gegenstandslose Welt" envisioned by Malevich as the radical possibility of abstraction, where all "things" will have "disappeared like smoke" once the "target of destruction" has been reached.[4] There is a "monstrousness" (*das Ungeheuere*) that transpires here, Heidegger says, which comes across if we juxtapose the Rhine as "built into the power plant," or literally, the *power*-work ("verbaut in das *Kraft*werk") and as "uttered by the *art*-work, in Hölderlin's hymn by that name" ("gesagt aus dem *Kunst*werk der gleichnamigen Hymne Hölderlins") (15/321). In this passage between

[...] In the cybernetic world, man too gets installed" (142). For a further discussion of these passages, see Bret W. Davis, *Heidegger and the Will: On the Way to* Gelassenheit (Evanston, Ill: Northwestern University Press, 2007), 179ff. In *Der Satz vom Grund* Heidegger develops this theme in relation to the principle of "sufficient ground" in Leibniz, and after noting that Leibniz was indeed the inventor of life insurance, he suggests that the project of steering and ascertaining eventually ushers in the transformation of everything to "information," and concludes: "Wir müssen das Wort in der amerikanisch-englischen Aussprache hören" (202). For a discussion of the connection that Heidegger establishes between Leibniz and cybernetics, see Renato Cristin, *Heidegger and Leibniz: Reason and the Path* (Dordrecht: Kluwer, 1998), 65f, 117.

4. "I have destroyed the ring of the horizon and escaped from the circle of things, from the horizon-ring which confines the artist and the forms of nature. This accursed ring, which opens up newer and newer prospects, leads the artist away, from the *target of destruction*. [...] *Things have disappeared like smoke*; *to gain the new artistic culture*, art approaches creation as an end in itself and domination over the forms of nature." Malevich, "From Cubism and Futurism to Suprematism," in *Essays on Art*, ed. Troels Andersen (Copenhagen: Borgen, 1968), vol. 1, 19. For Malevich's systematic account of "non-objective," or better "objectless," art, see *Die gegenstandslose Welt* (Mainz: Florian Kupferberg, 1980 [1927]).

the different senses of the work, the work of *power* and *force* and the work of *art*, Heidegger prepares the *constellation* of art and the essence of technology that will be the essay's final proposal.

This systemic, auto-regulating, and totalizing quality of enframing also indicates why man is not its subject, and it sets the limit for any instrumental interpretation: the subject no longer exists as an autonomous entity,[5] but is integrated into the reserve as the one called upon to carry out its operations. In this respect, man has a particular position, since he responds to the call of technological disclosure, and fulfills enframing. In this completion both man and being lose their metaphysical determinations—man as the *zoon logon echon*, being as the ground of beings—which is also, as will see, the key to why Heidegger can claim that enframing as such is the penultimate form, the "Vorform" of the event of appropriation, the *Ereignis* that will enable man and being to establish a new relation beyond metaphysics.

5. Which indicates the distance between Husserl's analysis of the relation between the abstractions of science and the life-world, and Heidegger: Husserl ultimately makes recourse to a transcendental subjectivity that founds both the life-world and all abstractions and idealizations, whereas for Heidegger, such a subjectivity has already been engulfed in the systemic auto-regulation of enframing. Husserl's solution, Heidegger might say, comes too late; absolute subjectivity as the ground of Reason belongs to the orbit of German Idealism, and was already superseded in Nietzsche. Moreover, for Husserl the emptying out of the deeper meaning of science occurs when it becomes a technique for the domination and control of nature, as this occurs from Bacon and Descartes onward, and loses its status as *episteme* in the Aristotelian sense of a "science that studies being qua being." For Heidegger the domination over nature is there from the start, and science and empirical techniques are both part of enframing. Technology, Heidegger says in "Die Frage nach der Technik," comes *after* science "historisch gerechnet," but science is, "geschichtlich gedacht," in its essence always already technological. If Husserl wants to save the "riddle" of objective knowledge from disappearing in a superficial technicity, and science as *episteme* from becoming a mere *techne*, then for Heidegger these relations must be inversed: it is *techne*, understood in the sense of a disclosure that includes epistemic and aesthetic relations, that harbors a "saving power," whereas the project of a pure *episteme* is already part of the will to power over being.

The "saving power" that Heidegger, following the lines from Hölderlin's *Patmos* ("Wo aber Gefahr ist, wächst / Das Rettende auch"),[6] locates in enframing, is dependent on our capacity to connect the various forms of posing and imposing in modern technology to their origin in the Greek *techne* and *poiesis*, and to show that they both are moments of *aletheia*, located however at opposite ends of the history of being. This connection is what allows us to move beyond the "correct" instrumental reading to the "true" one, and to see enframing as the final sending of being, where all of the possibilities of metaphysics are gathered together and exhausted, and where philosophy as such begins to approach its end in being gradually split up and absorbed in the different sciences (which themselves, as we have noted, may then be gathered together in the systemic theory of cybernetics).

It is in this context that we can see how Heidegger reworks some of the concepts put to use in his earlier thought. In *The Origin*, we find a connection between *Gestalt* and *Ge-Stell*, when Heidegger writes: "What is here called figure [*Gestalt*] is always to be thought in terms of the particular placing [*Stellen*] and enframing [*Ge-stell*] as which the work occurs when it sets itself up and sets itself forth."[7] In the Addendum, written in 1956, Heidegger suggests that this *Stellen* together with all of its cognates has to be understood in terms of a "letting lie forth" (*Hervorliegenlassen*).[8] Many of the statements in the first text imply something like an act of will, a positing that inscribes

6. For a discussion of Heidegger's use of Hölderlin and the legacy of German Idealism in the essay on technology, see Jennifer Anna Gosetti-Ferencei, *Heidegger, Hölderlin, and the Subject of Poetic Language* (New York: Fordham University Press), chap. 4. On the idea of a "saving power," see Otto Pöggeler, "Does the Saving Power Also Grow? Heidegger's Last Paths," in Christopher Macann (ed.): *Critical Heidegger* (London: Routledge, 1996), and Miguel de Beistegui, *The New Heidegger* (London: Continuum, 2005), chap. 5.
7. *Der Ursprung des Kunstwerkes*, GA 5, 51.
8. *Ibid.*, 70.

and produces a permanence, whereas the later comments move away from this dimension, which now appears to partake in the unfolding of technology as a mode of power. The *thesis* in the sense of "setting" (up and forth) should not be conceived of as a positioning emanating from subjectivity, Heidegger suggests, but as a letting-presence that cannot be reduced to the subjective modes of either activity or passivity. In this he intends to counter a possible misreading of the earlier text, although such a reading is not entirely without grounds.

This return to and rethinking of earlier concepts is also at stake in *Zur Seinsfrage*, where Heidegger returns to the reading of *Der Arbeiter* begun in the 1930s,[9] and, prompted by Jünger's essay "Über die Linie," which is the explicit point of departure, connects it to his current questioning of technology. The respectful tone of this exchange notwithstanding, it is obvious that for Heidegger the nihilism acted out in *Der Arbeiter* can only be taken as a symptom, and Jünger, in both his earlier and later work, is seen to remain on a descriptive level that does not allow us to think the essence of technology on the basis of Greek metaphysics, and thus even less to assume a *free* relation to it. The language spoken beyond nihilism, on the other side of the line that Jünger in his later essay proposes that we should cross, cannot remain the same, as if the step beyond would simply be a continuation of what has hitherto existed, and here too Heidegger sees Jünger as trapped in a metaphysics blind to its own presuppositions. Instead of simply going *beyond* the line (*trans lineam*), which for Heidegger simply carries on the project of metaphysics as a quest for power that aspires to create a new subject that would be master of technology, Heidegger proposes a reflection *on* the line (*de linea*) that meditates on nihilism itself

9. For a discussion of Heidegger's first reading in the 1930s, see Wolf Kittler, "From Gestalt to Ge-Stell: Martin Heidegger reads Ernst Jünger," *Cultural Critique* 69 (2000).

as the place where all the possibilities of metaphysics are gathered together. This line, Heidegger suggests, does not demarcate a territory that simply lies *ahead* of us, into which we could step by extending our current position, but it passes through us, and calls for a different kind of reflection on the *topos* where we are, a "topology" of being.

The overcoming of nihilism thus does not imply the disappearance of nothingness, and the return to an originary albeit lost plenitude, but a more thoughtful understanding of the absence, the *nihil*, that belongs to being itself, and which all of metaphysics has attempted to exorcize in its quest for power, ground, and presence. A full appreciation of this absence and this nothing means that being itself eventually must appear as "crossed out," both in the sense of a negative gesture that tells us that being is not a being, not a thing that we can claim or grasp (the metaphysical determination), and in the sense of a "crossing over" that points towards a transformed way of inhabiting the world, which is the explicit theme of Heidegger's writings on building and dwelling (to which we will return in the next section). This double operation of crossing (out and over) defines a "critical zone" where all securities are lost; yet we have to build something on this barren land, even though such edifices—and here we can gauge the distance traversed from the mid-1930s—can no longer be "houses for God or dwellings for the mortals," but can only consist in "building a way" towards a different thinking. The modern work of art repeats the Greek notions of *thesis*, *poiesis*, *techne*, etc., so that the original essence comes to shine forth beneath the modern technological interpretation of these concepts, both of which were still entangled in *The Origin*, where a voluntarist and decisionist vocabulary, based on violence and force was still operative. The constellation of art as the saving power hidden within technology in the later texts is fundamentally dependent on this connection.

The sending of being as technology is thus necessarily ambivalent, it is a "Janus head" that also contains the utmost *danger*, since it is an appeal to our *freedom*—we are claimed by the sending in such a way that a response becomes possible, where we think through the sending so as to become aware of the fact that enframing is only *one* of several ways to think being, and that being's disclosure both *needs* and *uses* man. We must not demonize technology, Heidegger cautions us, instead we should meditate on the "secret of its essence" as *simultaneously* danger and promise: the danger that we might simply accept technology and obey the call of enframing, and the promise that we may enter into a new relation to being by passing through the nothingness of being that technology brings forth, where both man and being shed all their traditional determinations and enter into the "oscillating domain" where a new relation between them can take place.

These two moments, Heidegger suggests, are like two astral trajectories both nearing and withdrawing from each other, just as (aesthetic) art and (instrumental) technology must seem infinitely at odds *and* yet intimately intertwined at the line separating completed nihilism from the other beginning. Thus there is a fundamental co-belonging of the dismantling of aesthetics, projected already in *The Origin*, and the release of technology from the instrumentalist interpretation, in that they both point toward the constellation of truth: the closer we come to the essence of *technology*, Heidegger claims, the more enigmatic *art* becomes, and the only way to experience this constellation is to abide within the movement of questioning, which is, as the final words of the essay read, "the piety of thought."

3.2. Building Thinking

Which, then, would be the essential features of a transformed relation to the world that would result from the thinking through of nihilism and the essence of technology? In many texts we find an attitude of waiting, listening, clearing a path, etc., but in other writings Heidegger also speaks more affirmatively of what such a way of inhabiting the world might mean, and this is where the connection to architecture and space becomes crucial. Heidegger here picks up some of the themes developed in *Being and Time* and other works from the 1920s, but places them in a new context, which is no longer that of a fundamental ontology. In the essay "Bauen Wohnen Denken" (first presented as a lecture in 1951), he addresses this relation to the world in terms of man's building and dwelling, and how these two components together allow for a different understanding of thinking.[10]

Just as in the essay on technology, Heidegger refuses a reading of building in terms of finality (architecture as a technical and/or utilitarian function), which, although it may be correct, does not give us access to the essence as that which grounds all relations of means and ends. The question bears on how building might make it possible for us to belong to a world, or whether this has in fact become impossible in the world of enframing.

Heidegger takes us through a series of etymological exercises

10. Recent discussions of Heidegger on architecture include Miguel de Beistegui, *Thinking with Heidegger: Displacements* (Bloomington: Indiana University Press, 2003), chap. 6; Karsten Harries, "Thoughts on a Non-Arbitrary Architecture", in David Seamon (ed.): *Dwelling, Seeing, and Designing: Toward a Phenomenological Ecology* (Albany: SUNY, 1993); Robert Mugerauer, "Architecture as Properly Useful Opening," in Arleen B. Dallery, Charles E. Scott, and P. Holley Roberts (eds.): *Ethics and Danger: Essays on Heidegger and Continental Thought* (Albany: SUNY, 1992). Since the late 1980s, an important part of the reception of Heidegger's writings on building has been focused on the re-working of his themes and concepts in Derrida and the subsequent possibility of a deconstructive architecture, which however falls outside the purview of the present text. For discussions of deconstructive architecture, see Mark Wigley, *The Architecture of Deconstruction: Derrida's Haunt* (Cambridge, Mass.: MIT, 1993), and Andreas Papadakis, Catherine Cooke, and Andrew Benjamin (eds.): *Deconstruction: Omnibus Volume* (London: Academy Editions, 1989).

that aim at showing how building and dwelling are connected, but beyond this also point to the verb "to be," which indicates that dwelling must be thought in terms of our human finitude, and as a way to protect that which emerges out of itself, i.e. *physis*. These connections have however become habitual, he suggests, and eventually forgotten, although not because of some human forgetfulness, but because of a withdrawal of language, a silence that cannot be *simply broken*, since it has *itself withdrawn from us* in the age of technology, and in this it is essentially connected to the nothing that belongs to being itself, and the *lethe* that is part of *aletheia*. We cannot simply overcome the negative by providing what is lacking, but only by over and over experiencing and accounting for the negative moment (a theme whose implications and various ramifications we will follow in the final section, in a discussion of the work of a paradigmatic modern architect, Mies van der Rohe).

In order to describe this finite human dwelling in the world, Heidegger introduces the concept of the "Fourfold," which joins heaven, earth, mortals, and gods into a unity. Here we can note how this aspect of joining together into a unity, where all parts reflect and receive their being from the others, signals a departure from the duality of earth and world in *The Origin of the Work of Art*, where this unity was understood in terms of a "strife" and a conflict. The Fourfold is presented rather as a "mirror game" (*Spegelspiel*). The earth is no longer the overpowering and self-occluding ground that aspires to draw the world into itself, but something that must be "protected," and here too we can discern a step away from the violence and power that is described as foundational for the *polis* in the texts from the 1930s.

In order to account for the stability and centered structure of this quadruple, Heidegger introduces the idea of the *thing*. Mortals, he suggests, protect the Fourfold by setting it into the thing, which is the essential role of building, and just as in the essay on technology, the example of the old wooden bridge is used to display how the thing gathers the landscape around itself in a non-coercive and non-impositional fashion. The thing is not added afterwards, Heidegger claims, but is itself the "gathering" of the four dimensions, and thus also a "spacing" from out of which particular places may emerge. In this sense, singular spaces do not emerge from a division of an all-encompassing and indifferent container, like the Cartesian *res extensa*, but are built up as it were from below, through the interplay of things and singular "locales."

There is to some extent a derivation operative here, and Heidegger sketches a genetic process, from Greek and Roman concepts of space up to modern n-dimensional spaces. His general point is however that the always present possibility of mathematicizing is not the transcendental condition of possibility for spatiality, but rather one possible *end result* that remains rooted in a pre-objective spatiality, which is neither subjective (belonging to psychology or to the mind) nor objective (mathematic or geometric).

Many of Heidegger's comments here run parallel to his own earlier remarks in *Being and Time* (as well as—more indirectly—to Husserl's account of the origin of geometric idealizations in the life-world), although the vocabulary of fundamental ontology and its analytic of being-in-the-world have here been displaced by a reflection that seems to begin from the world as whole, a unity to which *Dasein* (a term that here has disappeared as well) would belong, rather than include as one of its existentials. In fact, when Heidegger, at the end of his career, looks back to *Being and Time*, the question of space receives explicit attention, and he states unequivocally that the attempt in the earlier work to "derive the spatiality of *Dasein* from temporality is untenable,"[11]

---

11. "Zeit und Sein," in *Zur Sache des Denkens* (Tübingen: Niemeyer, 1976), 25.

which can be taken as an indication of the centrality of the issue in the later writings. Building and dwelling are in this sense essential for a different determination of thinking, where space and time must be understood as equiprimordial, whereas the second part of *Being and Time* sets for itself the explicit task of repeating all the spatial existentials in the first part on the basis of temporal projections.[12]

The essential dimension of building thus lies in the bringing forth of things that allow the Fourfold to presence, which for Heidegger is the true sense of the joining together, the *tikto*, that is the origin of archi-tecture as tectonics, and shares the same root as *techne*. Neither technology nor architecture should be understood as technological, but as a gathering, a joining-together, and an assembling that is a letting-presence and a letting-dwell—all of which is shown *via negativa* in the edifices of late modernity, which for Heidegger constitute a refusal or withdrawal of dwelling, but in this refusal also allow the question of dwelling to be posed with the utmost urgency. For Heidegger the uprooting of dwelling that characterizes the present moment (we should remember the situation of Heidegger's lecture, in the midst of the debates on the postwar reconstruction of German cities, to which he however pays little attention) is not just a mark of the present, but is rooted in the history of being and the advent of enframing; the "distress" (*Not*) is really an *absence of distress*, or a refusal to experience the silence and withdrawal of language and dwelling.

In one of his final comments on the relation between building and dwelling, the essay "Die Kunst und der Raum" (1969),

12. For a discussion, see Didier Franck, *Heidegger et le problème de l'espace* (Paris: Minuit, 1986). While it is undeniable that Heidegger's later works introduce many irreducibly spatial figures (*Gegend, Ort, Geviert*, etc.). I do not think that the question of spatiality as such is sufficient to account for the incompletion of *Being and Time*. I discuss this further in *Essays, Lectures*, 104–106.

Heidegger even more emphasizes the indeterminacy of our present situation, and the need for art to remain in a state of "namelessness." Discussing the art of sculpture, he claims that its specific spatiality, if it is to provide access to the truth of space, cannot simply stand opposed to the scientific conception of space that has evolved from Galileo and Descartes onwards, but must move into some other dimension, which perhaps does not even allow for a grounding of different and derived forms of space, but is marked by an as-yet-unnamable difference. Heidegger begins to unfold this theme in a reading of Aristotle's *Physics* and its analysis of *topos*. For Aristotle the *topos* always signifies something particular and not a general space, which first seems to pick up the thread from the earlier essay on building and dwelling, but then ends on a problematical note. If sculpture is an "embodiment" of primordial space, it is also true that it escapes all names: the term "volume" must "lose its name," just as the "qualities of plastic embodiment that seek locales and form locales would first remain nameless".[13] Thinking must here admit its *powerlessness*, Heidegger says, and sculpture can only give rise to a waiting, listening, and meditation on the part of the thinker.

If the sites of modernity are characterized by the flight of the gods, as was already suggested in *The Origin of the Work of Art*, and a withdrawal of language and names, then the namelessness of art would correspond precisely to our condition, where great art would be possible only to the extent that it is able to show us this condition, which in a sense was the answer that we tried to locate between the lines in *The Origin*. The question is of course what this namelessness, this void implies—to what extent we cannot avoid simply *filling it* by new forms of discourse, or

---

13. "Die Kunst und der Raum," in *Aus der Erfahrung des Denkens*, GA 13, 208.

whether this silence can be inhabited and endured in a different mode.

3.3. Conflict of Interpretations: Three Ways of Reading

The problem of how to assess, and make use of, the kind of reflections on technology, nihilism, and modern art that we find in Heidegger's later writings has deeply divided his interpreters. Here I will present three different perspectives, each of which attempts to develop different aspects of his ideas on building and dwelling: the theory of genius loci in Christian-Norberg Schulz, critical regionalism as it has been theorized by Kenneth Frampton, and finally the idea of negative thought suggested by Massimo Cacciari. In this section I will focus on the first two, since the work of Cacciari (and the Venice School of architectural critique to which he belongs) is central in the discussion of Mies van der Rohe in chapter 4, below.

It is true that Heidegger cautions us against any direct application of his thoughts, and that he stresses that a text like "Bauen Wohnen Denken" must be read as a contribution to the question of thought, and not as a sketch, no matter how preliminary, of a future aesthetics of architecture. However, as I argued at the outset, the task here is to confront Heidegger's thought with practices and theoretical work from the realm of the arts themselves, since, otherwise, the *Zwiegespräch* between art and philosophy would be essentially monological.

Another objection to the following would be that the dialog between *Dichten* and *Denken* is something that takes place in language, and in fact mostly occurs in relation to poetry, which not only is in tune with the fact that Heidegger even as early as *The Origin* presents poesy as a category that includes all the others, but is also evidenced by the sheer volume of his writings dedicated to literature, from the many lecture courses on Hölderlin, through the meditations on Rilke and Greek tragedy, up to a book like *Unterwegs zur Sprache*, with its extended discussions of the poetry of Benn and Trakl. In my reading, the case of building and dwelling seems however to engage in a more direct way the question of technology, in particular when it comes to crossing the line between the ontic and the ontological (to use terms that Heidegger no longer employs in his later writings). This is also why the impiety of many adaptations of Heidegger in this field should not be rejected as misuses of a pure philosophy. What Heidegger's thought in the final instance means is dependent on what we do with it, and there is no way once and for all to draw the line between possible uses and misuses.

Common to the readings to be discussed here is the loss of place as a point of departure in modernity, along with a divide between man and nature effected by technology, although the conclusions drawn are radically different, from visions of a return to a ground of meaning, to a synthetic and meditating theory of architecture as resistance, to a radical acceptance and affirmation of placelessness.

The first case, the work of Christian Norberg-Schulz, presents us with an aesthetic vision of an architectural practice that would counter the *Unheimlichkeit* of modernity by re-establishing the coordinates of a culture founded on nature, prolonging and confirming a *sense* that pre-dates human intervention. The place, he suggests in his seminal essay "The Phenomenon of Place,"[14] is a "total phenomenon," and drawing on both Heidegger's essays on building and his reading of Trakl in *Unterwegs zur Sprache*, Norberg-Schulz develops a phenomenology of space that empha-

---

14. Rpr. as chapter 1 in *Genius Loci: Towards a Phenomenology of Architecture* (New York: Rizzoli, 1980). The work of Norberg-Schulz, both as a historian and theorist, is multifaceted and rich, and I make no claim to do it justice in the following brief remarks; his reading of Heidegger is however well captured by this particular essay.

sizes architecture as a way to turn nature's own articulations into a human order. In Heidegger's reading, Trakl's poem shows us a series of relations between inside and outside, heaven and earth, private and public, man as a wanderer coming from the outside and the home as shelter, where the difference between them is organized by the threshold, which brings together "otherness" and "manifest meaning."

Norberg-Schulz develops this into a philosophy of landscape, where he attempts to show how it is gradually transformed, through architectural inventions that "explain" and "condense" it, from a natural setting to a meaningful place, which means to pay heed to a *genius loci*, or a "spirit of place." This is repeated in the edifice with its various tectonic details, which bring about a second gathering. In this way man can be said to *receive* the environment and *focus* it in his building, so that site becomes place in a series of acts that uncover a meaning already there in nature.

This conception of space and place draws on an idea of a sacred origin that Norberg-Schulz picks up from Roman mythology, where the environment was understood as wholly permeated by spiritual forces, a mythology of which he provides us with a secularized version. "Human identity," he claims emphatically, "presupposes the identity of place," and the priority given to movement and freedom in modernity must be challenged if we are to escape our seemingly irreversible condition of homelessness. Against the abstractions of science, architecture is a form of poetry, it allows us to, once more citing a formula that Heidegger picks up from Hölderlin, "dwell poetically on the earth,"[15] so that we may "cross the threshold and regain the lost place."

It seems that Norberg-Schulz's reading, while remaining faithful to the letter of many of Heidegger's statements, downplays the

---

15. See Heidegger, "...dichterisch wohnet der Mensch," in *Vorträge und Aufsätze* II (Pfulllingen: Neske, 1967).

unsettling quality that can also be detected in them, and that his emphasis on a plenitude of signification and sense, and on the integration of human works into a nature that already whispers meaning to us, wants to avoid the *indeterminacy* that for Heidegger has come to characterize the artwork (as we saw in the case of sculpture) in the age of technology. For Norberg-Schultz, it is as if this could be done through a new *aesthetic* that refuses to acknowledge the withdrawal and silence that Heidegger points to not just as some unfortunate development in modernity, but as belonging to being itself.

A similar aesthetic proposal is put forward by the "critical regionalism" advocated by Kenneth Frampton, which is the second reading of Heidegger that will be sketched here. Frampton's far-reaching and historically informed analysis of tectonics seeks to provide a mediation between the dimension of architectural form and cultural setting, and in this it gives a concrete richness to Heidegger's meditations on the Greek *tikto* and *techne*. Critical regionalism, as presented in the programmatic essay "Towards a Critical Regionalism: Six Points for an Architecture of Resistance" (1983), aspires to integrate this analysis into a theory of architecture as resistance, both against a postmodern eclectism and a pure technological universalism. Highlighting the regional, the specific, and the "place-form" understood in terms of topographic peculiarities, conditions of light and climate, but also tactile and perceptual elements like light and shade, touch and texture, it attempts to resist an increasingly homogenized universal civilization that mainly works through a propagation of architecture as image.

For Frampton, the dialectic of modern architecture reveals a tension between the representational and ontological, and he draws on the 19th century German architectural theorists from

Bötticher and Semper to Schmarsow,[16] although the conceptual opposition as such is derived from Heidegger. Tectonics is what transfigures materiality, while still preserving the earth, preventing it from becoming simply a reserve, as in Heidegger's enframing. In this it becomes the expression of cosmological vectors that organize our life-world, as in a slightly demythologized and architecturally more precise version of Heidegger's Fourfold, which Frampton derives from a reading of Gottfried Semper's theory of the "four elements of architecture."[17] Here the joint plays a crucial role (as an echo of Heidegger's discussion of *tikto*): it is an "ontological densification" that allows the other elements to come forth and acquire sense—an experience of sense that, Frampton says, must be understood as an interplay between connecting and disconnecting, joint and dis-joint that only together create a synthetic identity able to preserve difference at its heart.

If the first two readings each understand architecture, in their respective ways, as a kind of remedy, the third and final interpretation that we will address proposes something entirely different: a negative thought that emphatically denies that what Heidegger proposes would in any way amount to a return to an authentic world, or a nostalgia for a pre-modern unity of man

16. For a precise discussion of the origin of tectonics that comes close to Frampton, see Mitchell Schwarzer, "Ontology and Representation in Karl Bötticher's Theory of Tectonics," *The Journal of the Society of Architectural Historians*, vol. 52, No. 3 (1993). Tectonics, Schwarzer concludes, "can be read as an unresolved conflict between an ontological urge to regard structure as an irreducible essence of architectural form and a representational impulse to manifest built expressions through poetic commentary" (279). On the further development through Semper to Schmarsow, see Schwarzer, "The Emergence of Architectural Space: August Schmarsow's Theory of 'Raumgestaltung,'" *Assemblage*, No. 15 (1991).
17. See Gottfried Semper, *The Four Elements of Architecture and Other Writings*, trans. Harry Francis Mallgrave and Wolfgang Herrmann (Cambridge: Cambridge University Press, 1989).

and world. What is at stake here is rather to create an *authentic housing for inauthenticity*, to testify to the absence and impossibility of dwelling in the modern Metropolis. These are claims developed in the works of Massimo Cacciari and other proponents of the Venice School, and I will survey them in the next chapter, which is organized around a series of interpretations of the architecture of Mies van der Rohe, where the question of silence, withdrawal, and negation takes center stage.

4. Reading Silence: The Case of Mies

4.1. Mies as Paradigm Case

The fourth and final text of this thesis is a book entitled *The Silences of Mies*, initially announced in a footnote in *Essays, Lectures* on p. 356 under the provisional title "Mies van der Rohe: The Collected Silences." Originally intended as an essay, it eventually grew into a book of its own, where certain parts of the argument in chap. 7 of *Essays, Lectures* are developed in relation to an individual artist. But it also engages the more general question of the role of critical theory in contemporary architectural culture, which can be addressed as a series of responses to the claims made by Heidegger. As will become clear, this is also the place where the *Aus-einander-Setzung* with Heidegger takes the final step: the moment when the confrontation with works of art necessitates a going *beyond* the relation between modern art and technology reconstructed in the previous chapter, although not in order simply to leave it behind, but to come back to it from a different angle. What will follow here is thus neither a defense of, nor a criticism of Heidegger (and it does not pursue the question of whether there at all exists a Heideggerian perspective on modern art); rather it is an attempt to think through the complex of nihilism, art, and technology in its contemporary form.

The starting point, and the reason for the choice of this particular example, is the fact that the architecture of Mies van der Rohe has become paradigmatic for a certain tradition of critical theory, one that draws on Heidegger, but also on the legacy of the

Frankfurt School, often combining them in such a way that the analysis of technology is paired with reflections of the fate of art and aesthetic autonomy in the commodified world of late capitalism. A recurrent *topos* in this critical discourse is that of Mies's work as somehow silent: by situating itself at the limit of the modern tradition, at the point of exhaustion of the formal vocabularies of architecture, or even of artistic expression as such, it withdraws from the world into the sublime negativity expressed in the architect's own canonic formula, "beinahe nichts," "almost nothing"— a *nothing* that of course may be read in many different ways.

The underlying theme that connects the various sections in *The Silences of Mies*, which addresses a range of topics—the status of language in classical architectural theory from the 17th and 18th centuries, the role of glass and transparency in modernism, the use of silence in the plays of Samuel Beckett and the music of John Cage, and the theory of aesthetic autonomy and negation in Adorno in relation to the libidinal aesthetic in the early work of Jean-François Lyotard—is whether this idea of negation and withdrawal is able to account for the complex imbrication of art and technology that has characterized modernism throughout its history, for which architecture here serves as an example, but also an *exemplary* example. This final section comes back to the question of the avant-garde as a transformative event, where art does not simply negate its past forms in a quest for the new that would render its inheritance obsolete, but itself undergoes a metamorphosis by entering into contact with emerging technologies and social changes, and redraws the boundaries of subjects and objects, space and time. This does not imply that the ideas of negation, withdrawal, and resistance, as they have been handed down to us by a long tradition of critical theory, should be simply discarded, as some claim today, in the name of a "post-critical" attitude, but that they need to be reworked in order to be able to account for the complexities of the present.

Mies's first works can be seen within the context of what has been named "Die Streit um die Technik," i.e., the fight over how technology was to be interpreted in relation to a humanist culture of "spirit" and "values," which was a central topic especially in the intellectual life of the Weimar republic the 1920s and early 1930s, and within which the respective stances of Benjamin, Jünger, and Heidegger can be situated. For Mies, the initial task was to integrate technology with a classical formal language, or to create a synthetic "grosse Form" (which I would like to situate in the vicinity of Heidegger's question concerning the possibility of a "grosse Kunst," or what he in the first lecture courses on Nietzsche in 1936 referred to as "der grosse Stil"),[1] which aspires to the creation of a new monumentality attuned to the industrial age.

To attain the level of what the "spirit of the times" required, it is however necessary to reject the idea of individual expression, Mies claims, and to aspire for the pure rationality of the engineer. These two demands generate a conflict that becomes

1. For Heidegger, the grand style emerges in the coming-together of the physiological and the metaphysical as a *maximal tension*, and thus as a *highest unity*. It is only in the form of such a grand style, Heidegger suggests, that art can function as an antidote to modernity's nihilism. In the grand style we enter into the innermost physiological core of artistic creation, but we do so in order to *tame* it, to raise it up to a higher level of *form*. In this sense, if the physiological is required as a starting-point, this is because there has to be a tension that can be overcome in the fulfilled work. In this grand style we thus encounter the most profound chaos and the highest law, bound together in the work by a "yoke" (*Joch*). Here Heidegger's interpretation of Nietzsche in fact comes close to his own understanding of the work of art as the strife between earth and world, between an obscure and non-signifying element constantly withdrawing and turning away, and an element of signification and measure, and the *Joch* in Nietzsche here seems almost indistinguishable from the *Riß* in *The Origin of the Work of Art*. It is true that Nietzsche also calls this the *classical* style, and Heidegger does not object to this rubric, although he wants to distinguish it from classicism, which he connects with the tradition of 18th century German humanism, and instead suggests that we must look to Greek tragedy in order to understand the role of the "classical" in Nietzsche. See Heidegger, *Nietzsche I*, 146–62.

the driving force of the early work: how can a pure technological *Baukunst* (which Mies often opposes to the Beaux Arts associations of "architecture") integrate a will to form? The "spirit" is as it were made up of two parts that must be reconciled, and in some interpretations, most notably the one proposed by Fritz Neumeyer,[2] a synthesis is achieved in the late 1920s, where the forces of "Hegel" (striving towards an eternal order of things and absolute values detached from time) and "Nietzsche" (a belief in the primacy of will and a "plastic power" that creates new values) are united in a "bound duality," with the 1929 Barcelona Pavilion as the crowning example.

In this reading, technology makes possible a fusion of mind and nature, and also provides spaces for subjective aesthetic experiences that transfigure and spiritualize the technological and material dimension, as in the case of one of Mies's final works, the Neue Nationalgalerie in Berlin, where, as Neumeyer says, the "opposite worlds of transparence and gravity, of technology and architecture finally were united."[3]

Other readings have to a larger extent stressed the conflictual dimension of the early work, and located the final reconciliation at a later point. Particularly relevant in this context is the interpretation by Eric Bolle[4], since he connects Mies both to Nietzsche, Ernst Jünger, and modernity as a form of will to power based in technology, as well as to the idea of silence (which plays no role in Neumeyer), although in somewhat different ways than will be done here. Bolle points to how Mies's

2. See Neumeyer's introduction to his edition of the writings of Mies, *Das kunstlose Wort: Gedanken zur Baukunst* (Berlin: Siedler, 1986); on the Hegel-Nietzsche antinomy, 92-128.
3. Neumeyer, "A World in Itself: Architecture and Technology," in *The Presence of Mies*, ed. Detlef Mertins (New York: Princeton Architectural Press, 1994), 83.
4 See Eric Bolle. "Der Architekt und der Wille zur Macht: Das Problem der Technik in den Schriften von Ernst Jünger und Mies van der Rohe," *Weimarer Beiträge* 38 (1992): 390-406.

early work seems to strive for a domination over nature and a dissolution of the individual, akin to Jünger's organic construction, and to the presence of a strong voluntarist dimension. Like Neumeyer, he locates a period of doubt in the late 1920s, or more precisely a turn to an interpretation of technology as spiritual, although this is only accomplished in the late work, where the Farnsworth House (1951) holds the same reconciliatory position as the Barcelona Pavilion in Neumeyer's interpretation. Here, as Mies himself claims in an interview with Christian Norberg-Schulz, there is an "attempt to bring nature, houses, and human beings together into a higher unity" where they become "part of a larger whole."[5] The voluntarism of the prewar work here gives way to a "letting be," Bolle suggests, that brings nature and technology together in a harmony that comes close to Heidegger's idea of *Gelassenheit*. Strangely enough, Bolle's conclusion is that this release from the domination of technology *also* amounts to an absence and an emptiness, a Nietzschean pathos of distance from the world that imposes a "clear order on the Metropolitan chaos" precisely because it displays a "sublime contempt and indifference" toward it, and produces a "community that is based on mutual silence and estrangement." Even though the ultimate aim in both of these readings is reconciliation between man and nature, Bolle ends up with a vision of separation and division.

What is interesting here is however an idea whose ramifications we will trace in the following pages: the idea that the work of Mies must be thought of as *silent*—a silence understood in terms of negation, resistance, and withdrawal, but also as opening up a certain indeterminacy where critique passes over into affirmation, and where the dividing line between these two modes of thinking and acting becomes highly sinuous and labyrinthine.

5.   *Das kunstlose Wort*, 405.

4.2. A Brief Digression on Words

The idea of silence as an aesthetic option is of course dependent on an idea of architecture as an art that would not only normally *speak*, but also do so with a particular eloquence—and whose sudden withdrawal from language would thus be particularly significant and call for interpretation, perhaps for a "sigetics" (*Sigetik*), to use a term previously coined by Heidegger.[6]

The systematic use of the analogy between architecture and language dates from beginning of the 18th century, where it was deployed in order to determine the basis on which architecture could be taken as art. The framework of the comparison was provided by rhetoric, within which architecture could be understood as expressive and be linked to the hierarchy of literary genres and their respective subjects.

This strategy is also put to use by Charles Batteux, when he in his *Les beaux-arts réduits à un même principe* (1746) presents an almost completed version of the "system of the fine arts." The analogy with language is what makes architecture into one of the arts, while also assuring the superiority of poetry, the latter being a fine and free art in the truest sense. The most elaborate analogy between architecture and literature was developed by Jacques-François Blondel a decade later, but already here we may detect a worry that the architectural eloquence is about to be exhausted—which is in fact what half a century later would become the basic reason for the crisis of Vitruvian discourse, out of which the first signs of a modern vocabulary would arise. This crisis may then be understood as a moment of silencing, a kind of linguistic collapse, but it can also be understood as a transformative event, already full of nascent new discourses, where we move from a

---

6. On sigetics, see Heidegger, *Beiträge zur Philosophie*, GA 65, secs. 37–38. See also the discussion of Heidegger's reading of George, in Friedrich-Wilhelm von Herrmann, *Die zarte, aber helle Differenz: Heidegger und Stefan George* (Frankfurt am Main: Klostermann, 1999), §§27–28.

paradigm based on a representation of order, to one based on production and ordering, or from a mimetic discourse on nature to a type of discourse within which, as Heidegger would say, nature eventually will become a standing reserve.

In this sense, the "geometric silence" that a historian like Manfredo Tafuri (to whom we will return in the following) locates in the work of Durand at the shift between the 18th and the 19th century in fact is the birth of new discourse, impregnated by technology and the new authority of the École Polytechnique. This mutation, in which the mimetic orders were displaced by a logic of production, is a complex and multi-layered process where different languages *and* silences are intertwined, a prologue to modernity that can be read differently depending on the perspective that we choose to adopt.[7]

In this perspective, the invention of aesthetics also becomes a more complex phenomenon. The analysis of sensations and perceptions increasingly begins to focus on our sensorium as something produced, as resulting from an exchange between physiological conditions and external interventions. The theory of ideology and its repercussions in the architectural theory of Ledoux would be a typical case of this. If this is an *architecture parlante*, it is because it wants to transform our experience by providing us with a different sensory basis. Architecture here becomes a project in the sense of a *pro-jection* of a future order, and aesthetics, as a theory of a sensibility that from Baumgarten onwards begins to claim independence from the faculty of reason, has its precondition in the emergence of a subject that senses, feels, and is affected by objects in relation to which it pronounces judgments of taste, but it also, on a different level, entails the *production* of such a subjectivity, a new "distribution of the sensible," as Jacques Rancière

7. I sketch a brief interpretation of this shift in *Biopolitics and the Emergence of Modern Architecture* (New York: Princeton Architectural Press, 2009), 19–30.

says, which does not simply mean a rearrangement of entities that would pre-date this distribution.[8]

If this silence, which interrupts the eloquence of the classical orders and the mimetic paradigm, is in fact already teeming with other words, phrases, and vocabularies, how should we then situate the silence of Mies, located at the other end of the modernity that begins here? Does it signify that we here would have reached the *limit*, the critical line of the modern pro-ject, and if so, what would it mean to exceed this limit or line? In the following, I will attempt to show that this line is much more entangled and sinuous than it may at first appear (which will also take us back to some of the ideas developed in the earlier discussion of the transformational conception of the avant-garde), and will show it to be, just as the limit must be understood as *plural*, as a continuing variation and modulation, without any definite beginning or end.

4. 3. Negative Thought and Negative Dialectics

The analysis of Mies's work that established the paradigm of silence, negation, and withdrawal can be found in Manfredo Tafuri and Francesco Dal Co's two-volume work *Modern Architecture*, where it occupies a crucial position in the chapter "The Activity of the Masters After World War II." The authors here propose a reading of the fate of the European avant-garde, as it was gradually absorbed into the postwar corporate US culture and mutated into an international, placeless, and technological style. We are presented with several different endings of the heroic phase of Modernism, but the case of Mies seems to be most fateful and tragic in the sense that tragedy here becomes a conscious act, a supreme

---

8. See for instance *Malaise dans l'esthétique* (Paris: Galilée, 2004), and *The Politics of Aesthetics: The Distribution of the Sensible*, trans. and introduction Gabriel Rockhill (London: Continuum, 2004).

artistic achievement, and not just a waning of creative power.[9]

Tracing the development of Mies in his American period, in the design of the campus at Illinois Institute of Technology, The Farnsworth House, and other projects, Tafuri and Dal Co claim to discern a gradual reduction to facts, a division from the surrounding context, a "renunciation that makes it possible to dominate the destiny imposed by the *Zeitgeist* by interjecting it as a 'duty,'" carried out in buildings that "assume in themselves the ineluctability of absence that the contemporary word imposes on the language of form."[10] The pièce de résistance of this analysis is however the comments on the Seagram Building (1954–58), where all of the themes that structure the interpretation of architecture as an essential intersection of technology, modernity, and capitalism come together in a few dense pages.[11] Through a formal reading of the building and the way in which it sets itself apart from the surrounding city, Tafuri and Dal Co point to the "absoluteness of the object" and its "maximum absence of images" as a "language of absence" or a "void," which is then projected onto the city (or more precisely, onto the division that sets the edifice apart from the city) so as to form "two voids answering each other and speaking the language of the nil, of the silence which—by a paradox worthy of Kafka—assaults the noise of the metropolis" in a renunciation that here becomes definitive. The building interiorizes the abstraction of social life in late capitalism as its formal autonomy (or "absoluteness"), but in this it also casts a negative light on the metropolitan landscape.

This self-conscious tragic move—a language that silences it-

9. This chapter also discusses Perret, Gropius, Mendelsohn, Le Corbusier, and Wright, which all in their respective ways have to deal with loss of utopia that characterizes the postwar period. It is only Mies's renunciation, however, that attains the state of something tragic.
10. Manfredo Tafuri and Francesco Dal Co, *Modern Architecture*, trans. Erich Robert Wolf (New York: Rizzoli, 1980), vol. 2, 312.
11. *Modern Architecture*, vol. 2, 312–14.

self and withdraws from the world—then acquires its parodic counterpart (according to the famous claim by Marx about history repeating itself, first as tragedy and then as farce) in the proliferation of corporate high-rises that would follow in the wake of the Seagram Building, where tragic silence gives way to empty verbosity.

The above interpretation welds together a series of motifs: beginning with Marx, it mobilizes Kafka and Karl Kraus (both seen through the optic of Benjamin), Adorno, Heidegger, and probably a host of other thinkers as well. There can be no question here of attempting to do justice to Tafuri and Dal Co's interpretation of modern architecture in its entirety, which still stands as a major landmark in the historiography of modernism, or to the intellectual environment out of which their work grew.[12] The connection to Heidegger's analysis of technology may seem somewhat tenuous with respect to these particular passages (he is mentioned in other parts of the book, but not here), but it has been made by Massimo Cacciari, who at the time was a close collaborator of Tafuri. Cacciari discusses this in his review essay "Eupalinos, or Architecture,"[13] where he takes the reference to Heidegger as decisive for the project of writing a critical history of modern architecture.

12. Recent book-length studies on Tafuri include Andrew Leach, *Manfredo Tafuri: Choosing History* (Ghent: A & S, 2007); Rixt Hoekstra, *Building versus Bildung: Manfredo Tafuri and the Construction of a Historical Discipline* (unpublished PhD dissertation, Groningen University, 2005), and Marco Biraghi, *Progetto di crisi: Manfredo Tafuri e l'architettura contemporanea* (Milan: Christian Marinotti, 2005). As Biraghi notes, there is a whole typology of "silences" in Tafuri, and it must be seen in connection to the various forms of "fragmentation" operative in late modern architecture, the four prime cases of which are Mies, James Stirling, Carlo Scarpa, and Aldo Rossi. See Biraghi, chap. 5, "Il frammento e il silenzio." None of these studies however pays more than passing attention to the connection to Heidegger, even less to his question of technology.
13. "Eupalinos, or Architecture," trans. Stephen Sartarelli, in K. Michael Hays (ed.): *Architecture Theory since 1968* (Cambridge, Mass.: MIT, 1998).

Cacciari's interpretation begins from the idea of an uprooting of dwelling, a withdrawal of language, and the eradication of place, all of which corresponds to the negative moment in Heidegger's analysis. As we have seen, for readers like Norberg-Schulz or Frampton, this state must be countered by a remedy, be it the rediscovery of a *genius loci,* or of the mediated forms of tectonics. For Cacciari, the inverse is true: there is no return to an authentic dwelling, mediation must be undone, and what Heidegger asks of us is instead that we should learn to endure its absence as an irrevocable fate.[14] Heidegger shows us the *truth* of modern architecture, Cacciari suggests, the impossibility of the "Values and Purposes on which this architecture nourishes itself,"[15] and what characterizes his thinking is neither a nostalgia for some remote past, nor a desire for a future harmony, but a ruthless display of the insurmountable distance from the actual condition that marks all such discourses—including that of the semi-mythological Fourfold and the bridge over the Rhine, which for Cacciari appear as proofs *a contrario* of our inescapable modernity. This is also testified to by Heidegger's turn to poetry, which in Cacciari's reading preserves, although in the "non-being of its word," the lost tectonic element to which buildings can only "allude tragicomically."[16] It is true, he notes, that

14. On this point, the claims by Cacciari in some respect come close to the reading of Heidegger proposed by Kostas Axelos, who too understands enframing in a positive way. "The experience of absence," Axelos writes, "is perhaps the basic experience of the future. This new possibility of a clearing of non-being, this possibility of a new open world-being, this possibility of an understanding of being in play, is perhaps already a necessity, and corresponds to the distress of the world." *Einführung in ein künftiges Denken: Über Marx und Heidegger* (Tübingen: Niemeyer, 1966), 26. The difference is that for Axelos technology is what remains after the illusions of another thought (as in Heidegger's Fourfold) have been dispelled, whereas the proposal by Cacciari seems to be that the task of art is to bear witness to this condition of loss, and to create spaces that are appropriate to it.
15. Cacciari, "Eupaulinos," 394.
16. Ibid., 398.

Heidegger oscillates between the tragic and the nostalgic mode, although in the end, following Hölderlin, tragedy must prevail, as in Mies's "great glass windows," which point to the "the nullity, the silence of dwelling."[17] If Heidegger shows us the truth *of* architecture, Mies as it were does the same *in* architecture.

In other works, Cacciari has developed these ideas further, although he prefers to cite Adolf Loos as his main example. Here he also develops an idea of resistance, which seems to have little or no place in the commentary on Heidegger and Mies. In Loos the architectural project accepts its finite character, but in this, Cacciari suggests, it also opens up a "multiplicity of times that must be recognized, analyzed, and composed," so that "no absolute may resound in this space-time,"[18] not even the absolute of some utmost gathering of being's possibilities in enframing. This, he claims, is a positive and productive nihilism that must be accounted for in acts that are continually new, which is how he sees the paradoxically positive dimension of a pure "negative thought."

The tension lies here: on the one hand Cacciari wants to show that nihilism is the unavoidable outcome of modernity, on the other hand he wants to see it as plurality of languages, as in the case of Loos, which contradicts the logic of gathering and consummation derived from Heidegger. The readings of "Mies's silence" developed along this line point to the necessity of remaining within the *void*, within *nothingness*, whereas other readings would claim that this withdrawal must be understood as a determined *social* reality, as a moment of abstraction that is forced upon a subject that somehow must preserve the possibility of another relation to the world. Between them there is something like an *antinomy of*

17. Ibid., 404.
18. Cacciari, *Architecture and Nihilism: On the Philosophy of Modern Architecture*, trans. Stephen Sartarelli (New Haven: Yale University Press, 1993), 203.

critical reason: on the one hand, it seems impossible to be critical of the present without presupposing some form of redemption or reconciliation, no matter how indeterminate; on the other hand it just as much seems impossible to presuppose any such state of redemption without already giving in to an uncritically accepted metaphysical heritage. The dialectic, with its reference to a state of redemption, even if it is understood as negative dialectics in the sense meant by Adorno, appears, for Cacciari, as a nostalgic idea, whereas the proposal of Adorno's critical theory would be to see any idea of non-dialectical resistance as simply an effect of the abstraction of late capitalism itself.

The second interpretation, which draws on the Frankfurt School and the legacy of Adorno and Benjamin, will here be represented by texts by K. Michael Hays and Detlef Mertins, both of which attempt to insert the question of nihilism and technology in a dialectical analysis of capitalism and the commodity.

The two essays by K. Michael Hays that I will draw on, "Critical Architecture: Between Culture and Norm" (1984), and "Odysseus and the Oarsmen, or, Mies' Abstraction Once Again" (1994),[19] both address the possibility of a critical architecture that would propose a resistance to the world by way of an abstraction, where it both refuses to partake in social life and, in this very refusal, shows that it is necessarily conditioned by it: architecture interiorizes the social contradictions as contradictions inside its own form, as Adorno would say. Neither simply an instrument of culture, nor a pure autonomous form, architecture has a worldliness that mediates the exchange between the abstraction of metropolitan life and artistic form. Discussing the skyscraper projects from the early 1920s, Hays traces this dialectic between an architectural object that is open to reflecting the world while

19. "Critical Architecture: Between Culture and Norm," *Perspecta*, vol. 21 (1984), and "Odysseus and the Oarsmen, or, Mies' Abstraction Once Again," in *The Presence of Mies*.

at the same time remaining formally opaque, and that seeks to become a temporal event while still producing a distance from reality. This is further intensified in those later projects that seem to sternly refuse any participation in the fabric of urban life, and instead "open up a clearing of implacable *silence* in the chaos of the nervous Metropolis."[20] Similarly, in the Barcelona Pavilion, Mies creates a space of stark juxtapositions and contradictory perceptions, endowed with a temporal extension that calls upon the bodily trajectory of the viewer while still opening a "cleft in the continuous surface of reality."[21]

The second essay focuses on the later American work and analyzes the tension between the optical dimension (glass surfaces and façade texture) and tectonic structure (steel frame), and here too Hays locates a moment of resistance, where the work both claims a presence as an intrusive object, as well as undermines the authority of aesthetic experience, through the iteration of features reminiscent of the assembly line. Drawing on Adorno's distinction between construction and mimesis,[22] Hays sees in this an impulse to desubjectify aesthetic experience (construction), as well as, on the other hand, a necessity to make us feel and experience this loss (mimesis), which once more leads us, in Hays's words "to the silence, the abstraction that almost every analysis of Mies ends up

20. Hays, "Critical Architecture," 22.
21. Ibid., 25.
22. For a discussion of these concepts in Adorno, see Peter Osborne, "Adorno and the Metaphysics of Modernism: The Problem of a 'Postmodern' Art," in Andrew Benjamin (ed.): *The Problems of Modernity: Adorno and Benjamin* (London: Routledge, 1989); Peter Uwe Hohendahl, *Prismatic Thought: Theodor W. Adorno* (Lincoln: University of Nebraska Press), chap. 9; Andrea Barbara Alker, *Das Andere im Selben: Subjektivitätskritik und Kunstphilosophie bei Heidegger und Adorno* (Würzburg: Königshausen & Neuman, 2007), 418–436. Particularly relevant to the discussion of Adorno's relation to Cage in the next section is Alastair Williams, "Mimesis and Construction in the Work of Boulez and Cage," in Andrew Benjamin and Peter Osborne (ed.): *Thinking Art: Beyond Traditional Aesthetics* (London: ICA, 1991).

declaring,"²³ although not simply as a loss, but as that highest possibility of artistic language, where it allows the maximum tension between mimetic and constructive elements to unfold.

For Hays these tensions are however not so much an ontological as a social condition, which he describes in the wake of Adorno and Horkheimer's *Dialectic of Enlightenment* and its famous analysis of the siren song, where the dialectic between the artwork's sensuous density and plenitude, and its abstraction and dispersion, is mapped onto the structurally analogous process of abstraction in society itself. The *experience* of *abstraction* (where we have to hear the tension between these two concepts) in late modernity is materialized in the Seagram Building: it is what it *says*, by withdrawing into a silence that is the only way to keep the promise of language alive.

Detlef Mertins's interpretation, in the essay "Mies's Skyscraper Project: Towards the Redemption of Technical Structure," takes a somewhat different path, which seems closer to the proposals of Benjamin, in addressing the conflict of artistic and technological motifs. On the one hand Mertins sees in the early work a profound fascination with technological (American) modernity, on the other hand the quest for (European) constructive thoughts that resuscitate a discourse of "spirit," and would be underway towards a "transcendentalized substance of new artistic expression."²⁴

As Mies himself says, there is a need for "something more than just manifestations of our technical skill,"²⁵ and Mertins proposes that we should understand this surplus not as some additional ornamentation, but as a "transformative project,"²⁶ which in the early work had to do with making the technical structure aesthetic and natural, in the later postwar period became a way to make

23. Hays, "Odysseus," 237.
24. Mertins, "Mies's Skyscraper Project," in *The Presences of Mies*, 52.
25. *Das kunstlose Wort*, 298.
26. Mertins, "Mies's Skyscraper Project," 53.

us perceive the natural dimension of technology. For Mertins, the Miesian American skyscraper is both a spiritualization of technology and a materialization of a spiritual condition, which finally ends up in a tension between art and technology similar to the one was saw in Hays, although here expressed in terms closer to Benjamin, as a "melancholic contemplation, an acceptance of a condition of being resolutely divided from nature," which comes across in the act which transforms the "calculus of means and ends into the evocation of an end in itself."[27]

Whereas Cacciari wants the negative thought that underlies his cross-reading of Mies and Heidegger to remain infinite—irrecuperable—and thus in the end to constitute something that no longer can be understood along the lines of the Hegelian "negativity" that is a basic resource of critical theory, Hays and Mertins insist on the idea of a determinate negation, where the autonomy of the work is always bound up with the abstraction of the commodity as a social process. The resistance of the work must be exerted with respect both to the commodity and to the idea of the work itself as purveyor of pleasure, enjoyment, etc.—all of which eventually threatens to make critical mimesis and simple surrender virtually indistinguishable, so that what Adorno called the "Mimesis ans Verhärtete"[28] in facts ends up itself becoming something equally petrified and petrifying. The critical operation means to make this silence speak, or to speak in place of it; to invent a language that would be adequate to the withdrawal of language.[29]

27. Ibid., 66.
28. For Adorno too this is directly connected to a complex figure of language and silence, where the eloquence of the work only emerges to the extent that it respects what is *mute*: "Moderne ist Kunst durch Mimesis ans Verhärtete und Entfremdete; dadurch, nicht durch Verleugnung des Stummen, wird sie beredt." *Ästhetische Theorie* (Frankfurt am Main: Suhrkamp, 1970), 39.
29. The implications of glass and transparency are the theme of the following chapter (nr. 5) in *The Silences of Mies*, but since these discussions cover

4.4. A Multiplicity of Silences

But perhaps silence is not of one piece; the history of modernism displays a wide variety of strategies for resistance, withdrawal and negation of communication, the meaning of which remains highly contested. In this section I will highlight one particular interpretation, which is singularly relevant to the idea of critical theory, and also sheds light on the exchange between art and interpretative discourse that we pointed to above: a work that must excel in renunciation, and locate its operations where they become *almost* (echoing Mies's "*beinahe* nichts") wholly undecidable with respect to that order from which it wants to set itself apart (the essence of technology as enframing and/or the universal commodification of experience in late capitalism). This is the reading of Samuel Beckett's play *Endgame* proposed by Adorno in the essay "Trying to Understand Endgame,"[30] where the idea of a language that borders on silence as its ultimate resource is formulated in a particularly striking fashion. To this, I will here juxtapose another idea of a silence that no longer thinks in terms of negation, but understands it as a form of opening of language to the corporeal and affective, to a libidinal space that no longer knows any negation.

In Adorno's reading, Beckett's play approaches the utmost state of reification where it becomes impossible to separate *affirmation* from *critique*. To achieve this indifference is in fact the task entrusted by Adorno to Beckett, and he must follow it through relentlessly in order for the philosopher to extract a meaning out

---

        much of the same territory as the sections on Benjamin in *Essays, Lectures*, chap. 5, and the new themes introduced (above all the discussion of Colin Rowe and Robert Slutzky's theory of phenomenal and literal transparency) are peripheral to the argument here, I will move directly to a discussion of chap. 6 in *The Silences of Mies*.

30.   "Versuch, das Endspiel zu verstehen," *Noten zur Literatur*, *Gesammelte Schriften*, vol. 11; trans. Michael T. Jones as "Trying to Understand Endgame" in *New German Critique*, vol. 26 (Spring-Summer, 1982): 119–150.

of the text, which the text itself is strictly prohibited from ever naming. This meaning is however not something that philosophy as philosophy possesses from the start: it needs the work in order to reach this stratum of sense while still respecting the resistance that makes it into this particular sense. Understanding the play, Adorno writes, "can mean nothing other than understanding its incomprehensibility," which indicates that we are not within the logic of Hegel's *Aufhebung* of the work's sensible particularity into the concept, but within a negative dialectic for which "interpretation in its essence" must remain a "riddle."[31] Philosophical understanding always goes beyond the concept, and the work of art is that entity which is the most enigmatic and at the same time *more rich than reason itself*, or as he claims in another dense phrase: "The true stands open to discursive knowledge, but for this very reason it does not posses the true; the knowledge that is art, art also possesses, but as something incommensurable to itself."[32]

The historical accuracy of Adorno's reading of Beckett need not concern us here, since the point is to look into the underlying claim about the position of the work of art in modernity in general. Why, we might wonder, must the dismantling of language, the resistance to identification and literary recognition, seemingly a priori be understood in terms of negation and reduction?[33] Beyond the work of Beckett, minimal art and all

31. "Trying to Understand Endgame," 120, 122.
32. *Ästhetische Theorie*, 191.
33. Adorno's reading has also been challenged on philosophical and not just philological grounds. See the discussion in Simon Critchley, *Very Little ... Almost Nothing: Death, Philosophy, Literature* (London: Routledge, 1997), chap. 3. See also Deleuze, "L'épuisé," postface in Samuel Beckett, *Quad et autres pièces pour la télévision* (Paris: Minuit, 1992). Deleuze develops a reading that rehearses many of the *topoi* in Adorno, yet his conclusion is fundamentally different. For Beckett, he suggests, "exhaustion" is a *project*, and he aims at reaching a state where all possibilities are gone; he is indeed playing the "endgame," though not at all in sense claimed by Adorno. The first method of exhaustion is based in the language of naming, an "atomized, disjunctive, cut off, hacked up

its sequels would be a case in point where the idea of reduction seems partly misleading, since what is at stake is just as much the opening of the work to the whole of the spatiotemporal context, interactions with the spectator, and, beyond this, to investigations of various forms of institutional and discursive frames that condition our aesthetic responses.[34]

In order to gain a counter-point to the powerful reading of silence as negativity discussed above, we can confront it with another (or several other) silence(s), which can be found in the works and writings of John Cage. While this juxtaposition may seem overly literal and perhaps even simplistic, it in fact points to the precise line of demarcation beyond which the kind of negative theory that underlies the discourse on Mies's silence becomes problematic, or rather opens onto the *silences* of Mies, i.e. a reading

> language, in which enumeration replaces propositions, and combinatory relations replace syntactic relations: a language of names" (66). By naming all possible actions it ends up by immobilizing the subject. But the chain of words is infinite, thus also the need to exhaust words, and Beckett moves beyond the first language to a second one consisting of voices "which no longer move forward through combinable particles, but through intermingling flows. The voices are the waves or the flows which guide and distribute linguistic corpuscles" (ibid.). But exhaustion can just as little be attained in this language, which is the language of Others as possible worlds, since the series remains open and new voices will commence. Thus there is a need for a third language, made up of "hiatuses, holes, or lacerations which one would not take into account, attributing them to simple fatigue, if they didn't suddenly grow in a manner to gain something which comes from outside or elsewhere" (70). This third language, which Deckett develops above all in his television plays, finally leads us towards a pure Image, to a language beyond signification. This is however for Deleuze not at all to be understood as negativity or loss, but as the discovery of a positive dimension. As he suggests in the first volume on cinema, Beckett's project is to "regain a world before man, before our dawn"; see Deleuze, *Cinéma 1: L'image-mouvement* (Paris: Minuit, 1983), 100.

34. The critical literature on minimal art is vast; recent studies include Laura Garrard, *Minimal Art and Artists in the 1960s and After* (Maidstone: Crescent Moon, 2005); James Meyer, *Minimalism: Art and Polemics in the Sixties* (New Haven: Yale University Press, 2001, and Frances Colpitt, *Minimal Art: The Critical Perspective* (Seattle: University of Washington Press, 1993).

that opts for an irreducible plurality of modes.

My entry into this is through Jean-François Lyotard, who formulated this problem in direct relation to the legacy of Adorno's aesthetics, and as we will see, the reading of Cage's "several silences" plays a significant role in this exchange. Against Adorno's understanding of the artwork as "witness and martyr"[35] called upon to endure the burden of modernity, Lyotard proposes that we in the work should see a non-negative dispersal of fragments and intensities. This dispersal would no longer refer back to the lost totality of a whole subject or object, or to some kind of transcendental trace or lack (for instance castration, as in Lacan, or the process of deferring-differing, as in Derrida's *différance*), although it under certain conditions could form relative (w)holes. The events and intensities in Cage's works must be *bound* in order to become music, and such binding systems generate a depth, which however is something produced, and beyond which we find a pure energetics, the "matrix" or the "figural" that always overflows all discourse and all "figurative" form. In order for such a bound unity to appear, a kind of reduction is required, or a "desensibilization of entire sonorous regions,"[36] as Lyotard says, and it is only on this level that we encounter the idea of silence as withdrawal, i.e., as a particular becoming-insensitive to the plurality of events, or to the plurality inside each event, which is what produces the experience of a transcendental lack. Negativity, absence, and withdrawal are the result of a particular folding or manipulation of a surface, or several surfaces (the "libidinal band," Lyotard says), and they do not have the priority accorded them in that kind of critical theory Lyotard wants to leave behind.

For Lyotard this field of intensities and flows is an anonymous zone, it belongs neither to a subject nor to an object, and it can-

---

35. Lyotard, "Adorno come diavolo," in *Des dispositifs pulsionnels* (Paris: Christian Bourgois, 1980 [1973]), 109.
36. "Plusieurs silences," in ibid., 271.

not be said to derive from an immanent logic of the sonorous material[37] that would impose certain historically determine solutions. Instead, Lyotard suggests, it is analogous to the flows of capital, which allow for the co-existence of the most radical diversity and as such are fundamentally *indifferent to difference*. The very possibility of a critical theory is at stake here, and for the Lyotard of the early 1970s it has come to an end, at least to the extent that it would preserve a relation to Hegel and/or Heidegger, negative dialectics and/or the ontological difference. The problem with Lyotard's position is that it will eventually self-destruct as a position, and render the work of theory itself pointless or at least indifferent to the very idea of making a point. This is a paradox that Lyotard would face up to, and which later leads him to abandon his earlier work and move towards a new appreciation of Kant's critical philosophy, in order to address the problems of judgment and ethics that previously seemed foreclosed.[38]

37. This is what Adorno sometimes calls a "Tendenz des Materials," which he opposes to what he sees as a physiological, psychological, or phenomenological apprehension of the musical material, which all attempt to find some kind of "natural law." For Adorno there can be no constancy in the musical subject, not everything is possible at any given time, because the musical material is itself a sedimented spirit, shaped by society and history, which is what gives the law of the material's movement. To confront the material is thus always to confront society. This idea is introduced in *Philosophie der neuen Musik, Gesammelte Schriften*, vol. 12, 38–42, in the context of a discussion of Schönberg, and remained decisive for all of Adorno's writings on music. For a recent and thorough discussion of Adorno's admittedly complex and by no means peaceful relation to the works and theories of Schönberg, see Myung-Whoo Nho, *Die Schönberg-Deutung Adornos und die Dialektik der Aufklärung: Musik in und jenseits der Dialektik der Aufklärung* (Marburg: Tectum, 2001), on the notion of an "material theory of form," see Max Paddison, *Adorno's Aesthetics of Music* (Cambridge: Cambridge University Press, 1993), chap. 4.

38. This shift away from the Nietzschean, monist, and libidinal economy of the early work towards Kantian criticism and ethico-political reflections is undertaken in the name of the postmodern, which in this sense should not be construed as continuous with, or even less as an intensification of, the theme of the libidinal, as is often assumed. If there is continuity in Lyotard's work, it has more to do with the idea of a common zone between art and philosophy, and the necessity of developing

The possibility of interpreting Cage in this way[39] did not go unnoticed by Adorno, who commented on this type of aesthetic as a step toward an "informal music," long before Lyotard's intervention. In Adorno's perspective, Cage and his followers ascribe "metaphysical powers to the note once it has been liberated from all supposed superstructural baggage,"[40] which for him simply fulfils the destruction of the ego already performed by capitalism. As we noted, for Lyotard this destruction has in itself a positive content in emancipating us from subjectivity, and in this it in fact remains close to Cage, for whom the experience of the void and silence should be understood not as a loss of subjectivity, but as opening to other capacities for change: "self-alteration not self-expression," as he says in one of his last texts.[41] It is only by transcending (or in Lyotard's case, descending *below*) the model of consciousness and everything that is concomitant with it that we hear what is germinating inside these plural silences, inside this transformed music— although the question still needs to be posed whether this means that we have to discard the idea of critique, or, as will be argued in the final section, whether it points to the necessity of transforming the tools of critical theory without giving up its fundamental task.

> philosophical ideas by exposing them to the experience of art, or more precisely to that in art which questions our forms of experience. This is an attempt to locate a zone of *experimentation* that would belong to neither artist nor thinker, but constitutes their common "underground," as John Rajchman proposes in his "Jean-François Lyotard's Underground Aesthetics," *October*, vol. 86 (1998). I discuss the continuities and discontinuities of Lyotard's work in my "Re-reading the Postmodern Condition," *Site* 28 (2009).
> 39. An objection to Lyotard's reading would be that it uses a psychoanalytic apparatus foreign to Cage's aesthetic; the missing link might be Bergson, whose critique of negation was the direct source for Cage's first formulations of the impossibility of a pure silence; cf. Branden W. Joseph, "White on White," *Critical Inquiry*, vol. 27 No. 1 (2000), 106f.
> 40. Theodor W. Adorno, "Vers une musique informelle" (1961), in *Quasi una fantasia: Essays on Modern Music*, trans. Rodney Livingstone (London: Verso, 1992), 287.
> 41. John Cage, *Composition in Retrospect* (Cambridge, Mass.: Exact Change, 1993), 15.

4.5. Crossing the Line

The *topos* of silence can be taken as a sign of a larger complex of ideas, with which the fate of what has become known as critical theory is entangled. Interpreted either in terms of a negative dialectic that seeks to save the particular from subsumption under the violence of the concept (Adorno), or as a withdrawal of language that belongs to being itself in the age of technology (Heidegger)— figures of thought that for a long time seemed wholly opposed, but at present appear to share many essential assumptions,[42] above all the need for philosophy to constantly refer to art as the possibility of resistance to the present—it can be opposed to a different philosophy that understands silence, withdrawal, and negation as merely local effects, and aspires to move beyond the logic of critical negation, as in the case of Lyotard.

In the first option, silence and negation are understood as an ending, which may be interpreted in different ways: as the end of metaphysics, the tragic final gesture of autonomous and critical art in a world of commodification—Mies's *beinahe nichts* as the final word of dialectics or as the withdrawal of *physis* in the age of planetary technology. But would there not be a way to *pluralize*

42. Ever since the first systematic attempt to establish a dialog between Heidegger and Adorno, Hermann Mörchen's monumental and aptly entitled study *Adorno und Heidegger: Untersuchung einer philosophischen Kommunikationsverweigerung* (Stuttgart: Klett-Cotta, 1981), the literature on the topic has continued to grow. This connection can either be seen in a negative light, as in Habermas, *Der philosophische Diskurs der Moderne* (Frankfurt am Main: Suhrkamp, 1985), where these thinkers appear as ensnared in a philosophy of consciousness that prevented them from understanding the positive dimension of language in terms of a theory of communication; or in a positive fashion, as a task for a thinking that seeks to integrate both of them into an expanded critical theory (which is the proposal of the present text), which by no means excludes a critique of their respective projects. For recent examples of such readings, see Alexander García Düttman, *Das Gedächtnis des Denkens: Versuch über Heidegger und Adorno* (Frankfurt am Main: Suhrkamp, 1991), Andrea Barbara Alker, *Das Selbe im Anderen* (as in note 22), and the contributions in Iain Macdonald and Krzysztof Ziarek (eds.): *Adorno and Heidegger: Philosophical Questions* (Stanford: Stanford University Press, 2008).

such endings, to read them as points of passage and transitions, where future and past are both transformed—which also would mean to catch sight of our own present not as a belated echo, a vacuous repetition or parody, but as itself demanding an act of interpretation? This will be the final proposal here.

This reading will entail an understanding of the relation of nihilism, art, and technology as a field of constant modulation where none of these parameters is fixed, but each moves along with history. It does not imply any rejection of the critical as such, but argues for its continued relevance beyond any *specific* models of subjectivity and experience. These concepts must in turn be subjected to a historical analysis that acknowledges and accounts for them as ongoing processes of construction.

With respect to Mies in particular, and the transformed technological landscape in which his later work is situated, Reinhold Martin has proposed such an interpretation in terms of what he calls the "organizational complex."[43] He understands this as an aesthetic extension of the military-industrial complex, where architecture indeed still plays an important role, although not in the sense of a resistance or an autonomous art that would take it upon itself to signify an impossible redemption. Architecture, Martin suggests, should be understood as a conduit for organizational patterns, not just an image or an ideological screen, but more fundamentally as an active force that shapes and molds subjects, that "subjectivizes," to use Foucault's term.[44] On the level

---

43. *The Organizational Complex: Architecture, Media, and Corporate Space* (Cambridge, Mass.: MIT, 2004).
44. Foucault develops this theory in the later part of his work on the history of sexuality, above all with reference to Greek and Roman texts, and his vocabulary is shifting. He sometimes refers to this as a set of "technologies of the self," and even as an "aesthetic" of self-fashioning, which establishes a link to our proposals here. When he refers to the Greek practices as a "hermeneutics of the self" that would not relate to that which is "true or false in knowledge, but to an analysis of those 'truth games,' the games with the true and the false in which being is

of architectural history, this effectively displaces the question of
whether modernism has an end, where the initial utopian projects
were eventually abandoned, betrayed, or compromised, and instead focuses on the way in which older theories and visions were
reworked, taken apart, and reconfigured in order to become operative in a new complex of knowledge and power. The relation
between the two historical moments, the historical avant-garde
and its postwar repetition, would then not be something like a
break, a betrayal or a cut, but rather a transformation, and the
task of critical theory would be to account for the multiple possibilities for action and reaction that this process contains, instead
of assembling them into one unified movement approaching its
end. This is inherent in the transformative reading of the avant-
garde sketched in chap. 2 above: technological and social transformations are taken up in artistic practices that transform our
self-relations, as comes across most clearly in Benjamin's analysis
of technological reproducibility. This first appears as a destruction of aesthetics in a negative sense, a mere collapse of inherited

constituted historically as experience, i.e., as something that can and
ought to be thought" (*Histoire de le sexualité 2: L'usage des plaisirs* [Paris:
Gallimard, 1984], 12f), he is using a conception of the history of truth
that intersects with Heidegger's view of the history of metaphysics as
a gradual transformation of the different horizons within which beings
can be given in experience, where truth no longer means the correla-
tion between mental representations or propositions and states of
affairs, but a pre-objective and pre-subjective "openness" for all types
of subject and object positions, *aletheia* as the clearing in which beings
can be encountered. But unlike Heidegger's archaeology of thought,
which unearths those decisive philosophical moments in the history of
metaphysics where beings as such are given in new ways, the perspective opened up by Foucault's rereading of the *dispositifs* of sexuality and
the analyses of processes of "subjectification" and "technologies of the
self" allow other and more mundane practices than the strictly philosophical ones to play a constitutive role, and it makes possible a much
more stratified understanding of the subject and the domains of truth
in which it comes to relate to itself. For a comparison between Foucault
and Heidegger, and a discussion of interiority as a kind of "folding," see
Gilles Deleuze, *Foucault* (Paris: Minuit, 1986).

values (nihilism), but we should, pace Benjamin and Heidegger, understand destruction as the freeing of a "different element for the becoming of art," as Heidegger says, and for which the domain of *aisthesis* is not already there in an a priori opposition to the noetic, but itself results from our own practices. Aesthetics neither dies, nor lives on as a perpetually safeguarded zone, but is always reconstituted in relation to the other spheres of experience, which themselves are just as fluid. In this sense, "great art" (Heidegger) or "genuine aesthetic experiences" (Adorno) are those events in which the concepts of aesthetics and art are transformed and opened up, so as to become spaces of possibility, or rather, spaces of virtuality, where there is also a qualitative change in our perception of the past. Such events are moments when the inherited sense of art seemed to disintegrate ("from now on painting is dead"), but in fact was undergoing a transformation that made new and unexpected artistic practices possible.

Martin stresses that the transformation of architecture in the immediate postwar period was connected to the development of the discourse of cybernetics, and as we have noted, this type of systemic theory also forms the backdrop for Heidegger's perhaps slightly paranoid description of enframing as *ab-solute*, i.e. as a systemic loop of steering and securing that absorbs all exteriorities and outsides. But instead of an absolute that gathers together all the moments of history into a final phase that absorbs the subject into the standing reserve, and eventually engulfs philosophy itself, would it not be possible to understand this as the formation of other subjectivities and possibilities of experience, including aesthetic ones that take these experiential modes as their point of departure? For Heidegger, the end of philosophy that places us before the task of thinking occurs at this moment, just as the possibility of a genuine aesthetic experience for Adorno was transformed into a negative utopia that can only be kept alive in the utmost negation of this experience. A different reading of this moment may allow us to come back to these all too apocalyptic gestures, to disentangle them from the perception of their own moment as the final one, and make them productive once more in our present, by stressing the moment of indeterminacy that they contain, an indeterminacy that is of the order of the virtual (which is perhaps how we should understanding Cacciari's reading of nihilism in Loos as an opening toward "multiplicity of times that must be recognize, analyzed, and composed").

In this shift, critical theory itself seems to be *on the line*—but what is such a line? Can we simply move beyond it, or should we assume, as Heidegger does in his exchanges with Jünger, that this line does not delimit a space that would simply extend before us and that we could enter into, but that it *runs through man himself*? Using Heidegger's image, we might conclude that such a shift is both close to and far from Heidegger's own understanding of the line, which still remains entrenched in the idea of an end of metaphysics as a final gathering of all possibilities into a highest conflictual unity.

The conclusion would be the following: we cannot simply leave critical theory behind, yet neither can we continue to use the concepts that it has bequeathed to us. Adorno famously notes in the draft for an introduction to *Ästhetische Theorie* that the very expression "'philosophical aesthetics' gives the impression of something outdated."[45] Rather than a confession of failure, this is a precise indication of the fact that all critical-theoretical reflections *themselves belong to time*, and must move with it, which Adorno was the first to admit, and which is one of the founding premises of his aesthetic theory. Similarly, if many of the proposals in Heidegger's analysis of technology appear in dire need of a confrontation with contemporary developments, and the assumed independence of technology's essence from actual tech-

---

45. *Ästhetische Theorie*, 493.

nology must be questioned, such a questioning in fact belongs to the movement of thought itself, and is a sign of fidelity rather than rejection. The highly insecure status of concepts like Nature and the Subject, which have functioned like the regulative ideas of critical theory, should then not lead us to despair, nor to any simplistic rejection of critique as such. If we instead assume that nature and subjectivity, and finally being itself, as the horizon against which all such concepts are understood, necessarily move together, not in parallel, but in parallax, then the loss or waning of certain categories should not be confused with any end of critique as such. The task of theory remains as important as ever, and what we earlier formulated as the antinomy of critical reason should then not be seen as heralding its end, but as the sign of a necessary transformation.

www.ingramcontent.com/pod-product-compliance
Ingram Content Group UK Ltd.
Pitfield, Milton Keynes, MK11 3LW, UK
UKHW022209230426
12048UKWH00016BA/741

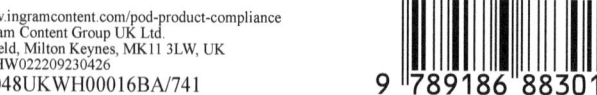